Robin Lloyd-Jones grew ___
He has served as President ___ ___riters
(1993–1996) and the Scottish ___ ___ional (1997–
2000) and has also taught Cre ___ ___lasgow University.
His book *The Sunlit Summit* ___ ___re Society Research Book
of the Year Award in 2013 and his novel *The Dreamhouse* was
nominated for the Booker Prize in 1985.

Other books by Robin Lloyd-Jones

Fiction
Red Fox Running (Anderson Press, 2007)
Fallen Angels (Canongate, 1992)
The Dreamhouse (Hutchinson, 1985)
Lord of the Dance (Gollancz and Arena, 1983)
Where the Forest and Garden Meet (Kestrel, 1980)

Non-fiction
Fallen Pieces of the Moon (Whittles Publishing, 2006)
Scottish Wilderness Connections (Rymour Books, 2021)
The New Frontier (Thunder Point Publishing, 2019)
Autumn Voices (Play Space Publishing, 2018)
The Sunlit Summit (Sandstone Press, 2013)

Radio Drama
Rainmaker (BBC radio drama, 1997)
Ice in Wonderland (BBC radio drama, 1993)

ARGONAUTS
OF THE
SCOTTISH ISLES

Sea-kayaking Adventures

Robin Lloyd-Jones

BIRLINN

This edition published in 2022 by
Birlinn Ltd
West Newington House
10 Newington Road
Edinburgh
EH9 1QS

www.birlinn.co.uk

ISBN 978 1 78027 705 9

British Library Cataloguing-in-Publication Data
A catalogue record for this book is available
on request from the British Library

Papers used by Birlinn are from well-managed
forests and other responsible sources

FSC
www.fsc.org
MIX
Paper from
responsible sources
FSC® C018072

Typeset by Hewer Text UK, Edinburgh
Printed and bound by Clays Ltd, Elcograf S.p.A.

Contents

List of Maps

Introduction

Argonauts of the Western Isles was first published in 1989 by Diadem Books. Then, in 2008, Whittles Publishing put out an edition containing an extra five chapters covering my kayaking adventures on the Scottish west coast since the original version. With the addition of some fresh photographs, this current edition by Birlinn has the same content as the 2008 version, but is in a smaller, more compact format and with the slightly different title of *Argonauts of the Scottish Isles*. The fact that the book has not been out of print for over thirty years says much for the lure of Scotland's remote islands and wild shores. It is my hope that this latest edition will introduce new generations to the adventure and joy to be had in these wilderness places.

Readers should bear in mind that some of the adventures described in the early chapters might be nearly sixty years in the past. When you read the word 'now', it refers to a historical kind of now. Equipment and techniques have changed over the years and much of the advice offered in the earlier chapters is out of date. However, I have not altered any of this because I think there is value in letting it stand as a record of how things used to be done. In the intervening years there has been a much greater emphasis on safety. There are parts which at the time seemed like grand adventures, but now read more like cautionary tales.

One obvious change is that there is a lot more sea kayaking being done these days. Kayaks on top of a car used to be an unusual sight. Now you see them everywhere. New and more efficient kayaks and paddles, improved clothing, instant tidal predictions off the Internet, and satellite navigation have all made life easier. I am amazed at the discomfort I was prepared to put up with in the old days. Better equipment has helped push up the standards of performance. So too has the coaching efforts of the kayak clubs, assisted by the British Canoe Union and the Scottish Canoe Association. Routes which were regarded as fairly advanced in days of yore are all in a day's work for the average modern paddler. And talking of changes – like the mountains, which for some strange geological reason are becoming steeper with the passing years, I'm sure the sea is getting colder and my kayak heavier!

Most of the places described I have returned to several times over. Each time is a new experience. The weather, the tide, my companions are different, and I myself see things through different eyes. I visit the wreck of the *Captayanis* regularly. Like me, it gets a little rustier each year.

I would like to thank my friends Archie, Martin, Michael, Ian and Colin, whose companionship has doubled the pleasure of all those miles paddled. My profound gratitude goes to all the moments and places recorded in this book and the many unrecorded incidents too which have refreshed and recharged me in body and spirit.

I will end by quoting from the Preface to the 1989 edition. With the environment increasingly under threat and now that I have grandchildren, the words mean even more to me than before:

> In spreading the word about remote and beautiful spots am I hastening their destruction? I think not. Those who reach them using only paddle or sail have experienced a closeness to nature. They know such riches are worth preserving. It is my hope that this book will increase the number of voices in favour of conservation so that the islands and coasts I describe are still unspoilt when our children's children beach their kayaks on their shores.

Robin Lloyd-Jones
Helensburgh
January 2022

Chapter 1

The Start Of A Long Affair

Induction and training

When I was five years old, my aunt, recently returned from Canada, assured me that Red Indians parted their hair down the middle in order to balance their canoes. From that day on I had been quite convinced canoes were tippy, unreliable things. So, years later in the 1960s, I was dismayed to find myself taking part in a canoe expedition. Under the impression that I was the instructor of mountaineering, camping and general hillcraft, I had arrived at the Outward Bound Moray Sea School near Elgin in Scotland only to be told that I was scheduled to lead a group on a grand circular expedition which included not only a four-day walk across the Cairngorms (never seeing more than about ten feet ahead of us the whole time because of thick mist), but also 100 miles of cycling, a journey in small boats up the west coast, the rounding of Cape Wrath in the sail-training ship the *Prince Louis* and a canoe trip from one side of Scotland to the other via the Caledonian Canal which links the Moray Firth on the east coast to Loch Linnhe on the west coast by way of Loch Ness, Loch Oich and Loch Lochy. 'But I've never sat in a canoe in my life!' I protested. 'If you're officer material you can lead anything,' was the reply. Another favourite saying of the course commandant was, 'Instructors are expendable, punters aren't.' Like an eighteen-inch welly boot in nineteen inches of water, I was filled with cold dread at the thought of being expended in one of those dangerous vessels. The leader was really a 'punter' in disguise. The expedition was preceded by ten days of training, much of which was aimed at fostering teamwork. For this reason all the canoeing was done in double canoes and the rescue drills were specially designed to involve the whole group. In retrospect, I realise I didn't learn much that was subsequently of use to me as a reasonably serious sea kayakist, but it whetted my appetite. I had felt the bows lift to a wave, I had felt the sea rolling beneath me and become part of its rhythm. Sitting a few inches below its surface, separated from it only by the thickness of a skin, I experienced an intimacy with the ocean I had known in no other craft – every wave individual, every motion communicated, man and sea with a minimum of technology between. In short, I was hooked for life.

They say that camping is the severest test a marriage can undergo. Couples still wishing to prove a point should try a longish trip in a double canoe. The guy in the bows becomes convinced he is doing all the graft, imagines his partner behind him sitting back enjoying the scenery. Meanwhile, the fellow in the stern is working up a real hatred for the back of the neck and the silly ears which, mile after mile, have been blocking his view, and for the stupid owner of them who is setting a pace that is either too fast or too slow and who is obviously to blame for the fact that the two paddles keep clashing. Not surprising, therefore, that halfway up Loch Lochy one of our group suddenly let out an anguished cry, stood up in the canoe and brought his paddle down on the head of his unsuspecting partner.

Shortly after this summer holiday job as an instructor, I changed schools and took up a new teaching post in Helensburgh, a seaside town on the Firth of Clyde. The house which I shared with my wife, three children and six cats was on the water's edge. When the tide was up the sea was only two feet away from the end of the garden – ideal for canoeing. Furthermore, the new school, Hermitage Academy, had amongst its staff a compatible soul, an art teacher named Archie. What neither of us had was a canoe, nor the money to buy even second-hand ones or kits. Then, one lunch hour, we decided to sunbathe on the roof of the four-storey school building. Archie had found a way up to it and a key that fitted a locked door. In a corner of the flat roof, sheets of discarded asphalt material were hiding something. If the thickly made fibreglass effort we uncovered wasn't a bath it must be a double canoe. Together we could hardly lift it. Then, as we removed more of the asphalt, we came across two single kayaks. One was a wooden framework with a thin PVC material stretched over it. Its ribs were fractured, its skin cut and torn. Archie fingered the shiny, wet-look PVC.

'You're the kinky one, this had better be yours.'

The other had been assembled, none too expertly, from a plywood kit. It too was holed and splintered.

Nobody seemed to know anything about the canoes or care whether we made use of them or not. So, the next day, with the aid of our climbing ropes, we lowered the two singles over the edge. Unfortunately, the kinky canoe took a dive from two storeys up onto the tarmac below.

'This puts Cilla Black's nose-job in the shade!' Archie commented.

Several weeks and a great deal of repairing later, came the moment of the launch from the end of my garden. We wore windproof anoraks, T-shirts, shorts and canvas shoes. Welly boots, I had read somewhere, were dangerous, they could fill up with water and drag you down. It was several years before I questioned this myth, several years of canoeing with wet feet quite unnecessarily. For life jackets we sported thick kapok things which had come from the lifeboat of some liner which was being dismantled in the breakers' yard at Faslane on the nearby Gareloch. Sallie, my wife, kissed the patched bows of my kayak. Archie struck a heroic pose, raised a bottle of whisky and quoted:

> The sea wants to know – not the size of your ship,
> Nor built with what art;
> Nor how big is your crew, nor your plans for the trip
> But how big is your heart.

We took a slug each, then lifted our craft into the water.

I, of course, was the expert. That is to say, I had actually been in a canoe before. I showed Archie how to get in by sitting on the stern with the homemade paddle out to one side as a stabiliser. We wobbled out into Helensburgh Bay, getting used to the feel and balance of our kayaks. Novice and complete beginner though we were, in fact, we possessed already a fair amount of relevant skills and knowledge. My father had been a keen yachtsman, keeping a boat in Dartmouth and sailing to places like the Channel Isles, Cherbourg, the Isle of Wight. I knew something about the habits of the sea, the tides, a little about navigation and charts and I was used to having an oar in my hand. It still takes me by surprise when I encounter learners in a canoe who haven't grasped the basic principle of which side you paddle if you want to turn, or that paddling in reverse produces the opposite effect.

Archie, too, had grown up near the sea and was used to the ways of small boats. And both of us were mountaineers. We knew about hypothermia and the general clothing and calorie needs of the body in hard outdoor situations; we knew about camping and compass work; and we knew that safety and survival were matters to be taken seriously. Above all, through mountaineering, we had discovered the satisfaction of accepting the challenges posed by rugged terrain or difficult natural conditions, of being self-reliant, the joys of exploration, the magnificence of wild and lonely places, the fulfilment and refreshment of spirit that a day in such an environment can bring. To us, these two old and much-repaired kayaks were a means to an end, a means of reaching further into the unspoilt places, of extending these kinds of experience, of getting to know the sea in the same way that we knew the ever-changing moods of the mountains of Scotland, and of journeying in one of the most exciting zones the earth can offer – the zone where the elements of land and sea perpetually war with each other.

People enjoy canoeing for reasons ranging from masochism (or is it machoism?) to communion with the gods. Although I have certainly found satisfaction in mastering the techniques and in being able to match my skill and training against the forces of nature, the end rather than the means has always remained the most important thing to me. Whatever your reasons, finding like-minded companions is essential and, in Archie, I had found someone whose attitudes and motivation exactly matched my own. Not that any of this would have been apparent from that first hesitant circumnavigation of Helensburgh Bay. Somewhere out in the middle of the bay Archie said, 'What about buoyancy?'

'What?'

'I doubt if the natural buoyancy of either of these is sufficient for them to keep afloat if they fill up with water.'

'My God! I never thought of that! Quick! Part your hair down the middle!'

Ever since then I have always checked any canoes in my group to make sure there's something in bow and stern – air bags, old life jackets, blocks of polystyrene, well-capped empty plastic bottles – to keep them afloat. It's amazing how the obvious can be overlooked.

The following weekend we decided on a rather longer trip, but one which we thought would be much safer since it was down the placid river Leven, with neither bank too far away. In its own way, it turned out to be a trip full of hazards. The plan was to launch about eight miles upriver at Balloch where the Leven flows out of Loch Lomond towards Dumbarton on the tidal estuary of the Clyde. The first hazard was a group of teenagers in hired dinghies with outboard motors who decided to 'buzz' us. Disdainful unconcern failed. Plan B was to beat it as fast as possible. It was a question of which overheated first, their puny put-put engines or us. Luckily their time must have been up because they suddenly turned round and headed back to Balloch.

Then came a stretch of countryside and, in a particularly shallow section, a herd of cows, knee-deep – do cows have knees? – blocking our way.

'Just think of them as slalom gates,' Archie said, heading for the underbelly of a fat Friesian. I wish, for the sake of the story, I could say that he passed between its legs, or that we were holed by a pair of longhorns. The best I can say is that, in a sea kayak, you expect the odd dropping from a seabird to defile your deck, but not . . . Anyway, my death-wish for some kind of spectacular holing was fulfilled by a submerged reef of rusty bedsteads. On the bank I taped up the rip in my PVC while Archie held at bay the pack of wild dogs that run free on most housing estates in these parts.

Hardly had we got going again when a horde of pint-sized cowboys ran along the bank, whipping imaginary horses and pointing sticks at us while making firing-type noises and shouting, 'The last of the Mohicans!'

Stupidly, I raised my paddle as if it were a bow and loosed off a few arrows at them. The response to this was a hail of stones, nothing imaginary about them. This fusillade was maintained for several hundred yards until the two Mohicans finally outstripped them.

There remained the hazard of the bridges. At the first bridge we could be seen approaching from a long way off.

'Bombs away!' someone shouted.

The bricks narrowly missed us, sending up columns of spray as in *Sink the Bismarck*. The second bridge was soon after a bend and we were merely spat upon. By the third bridge we were sadder and wiser men, paddling slowly till the last moment, then spurting with a change of angle as we passed beneath it. The fourth and last bridge contained an unexpected surprise. There was a small waterfall where there hadn't been one when I did my

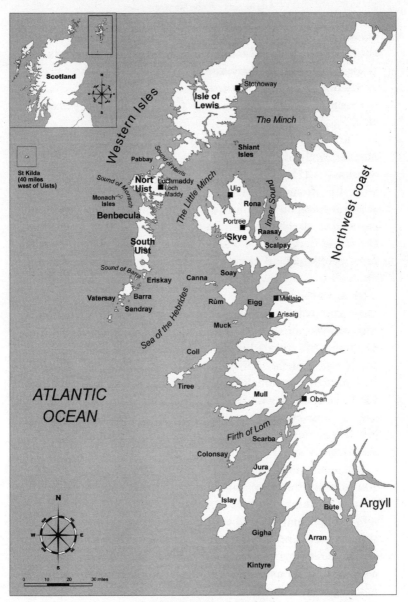

The Western Isles of Scotland

reconnaissance – the difference between the level of the river and the tidal waters beyond at high and low water. Allowing ourselves to be swept over the three-foot drop we drifted to the quayside where our pick-up car awaited us.

'Stick to the sea,' Archie said. 'Come wind, come storm, it's safer!'

Our trips became longer, but always remained within the comparatively sheltered waters of the Clyde Estuary and its adjoining sea lochs. We realised the benefits of spray decks which, worn like skirts and fitted over the cockpit, keep out breaking waves and keep in body heat; and we discovered that a good foot-rest makes all the difference to paddling – a solid base enabling the whole weight of the body to be put into the stroke. As with most people unused to paddling, it took both of us a while to appreciate that the pushing muscles of the arm, shoulder and back are stronger than the pulling muscles and that paddling is more a matter of punching the raised blade forward than of pulling the lower blade back through the water. And we discarded our bulky life jackets for slimmer borrowed ones, more appropriate to paddling, which could be inflated if required. Incidentally, occasionally I observe novices fully inflating their life jackets at the start of an outing. This is not advisable, not only because they are then too bulky for comfortable paddling, but also because, in the event of a capsize, that amount of buoyancy can press a person hard up against the underside of the canoe, making exit difficult. The proper time to inflate it is once you're out of the canoe and a long wait in the water seems likely. Strictly speaking, this type of jacket is a buoyancy aid until it is inflated and only then does it become a life jacket capable of supporting the head of an unconscious person above the waves. There's a rather grim joke that the difference between a buoyancy aid and a life jacket is that with the latter your dead body is still afloat when it's found.

Once we felt reasonably competent, Archie and I went to our headmaster and asked for funds to start a canoe club in the school. He agreed, on the condition that we went on an approved course and gained our proficiency certificates and instructor's certificates for sea kayaking. The education authority would pay the cost. Thus it was that we found ourselves at the Inverclyde National Recreation Centre at Largs on the Ayrshire coast, on one of the regular courses for the proficiency certificate run by the Scottish Canoe Association.

The course was quite an eye-opener. The less you know the less you realise how much more there is to know. Socrates is reputed to have said that he was the wisest person in the world because he alone knew that he knew nothing. Well, for us, this was the beginning of wisdom. For a start, we were in kayaks that performed so much better than our own, that behaved better in crosswinds and running seas and manoeuvred more easily. Up till this point, a kayak was just a kayak. Now we saw that its design was an important consideration. And then there were the deep-water rescue techniques for getting a capsized person back into his or her kayak. It came home to me that, prior to this, my notion of what to do had been very inadequate indeed. Had either Archie or myself capsized in deep, rough water before going on this course we could well have been in a lot of trouble. It seems incredible now, but neither of us had thought to try out a rescue in shallow water. We had assumed that, if an emergency arose, we would muddle through somehow. Maybe Archie had more faith in me as 'the expert' than I deserved. Another revelation was the whole range of support strokes and draw strokes. I'd had no idea that it was possible to lean on the water with your paddle blade and to push yourself upright again or to make a canoe move sideways. Ian, our instructor, demonstrated that it was possible to lean the canoe over until his ear was in the water and still recover to an upright position. He also demonstrated rolling a kayak. This was not part of the course, but I decided that I would make every effort to master the art as soon as possible. The most valuable thing I learned from Ian was that brute strength is never a substitute for good technique. A seven-stone woman, with good technique, should be able to empty and right a canoe with a hundredweight or more of water in it. With good technique and timing one can roll up a fully laden kayak almost effortlessly.

Whilst trying all these new strokes, I was averaging about five capsizes a day.

'Stick to the sea, it's safer!' Archie would shout every time my head emerged above the waves.

'It's the ones who aren't capsizing that I worry about,' Ian said. 'It means they're being too timid, they're not pushing themselves to the limit, not trying to extend themselves.'

'What if I capsize during the test itself?' I asked.

'You won't be penalised for trying too hard . . . as long as you come up smiling. It's only the ones who break the surface with panic on their faces who are failed.'

'As long as you come up smiling!' became the catchphrase for the course.

This was before the days of kayaks with watertight compartments and bow and stern hatches, so the correct packing of a canoe for a camping trip was an important aspect of the certificate. Part of the test was to pack the kayak as for such a trip, with everything properly wrapped and protected against the sea, then paddle out and capsize. If, on landing, any item of gear was wet, you had failed.

It was like a catechism:

'What is the correct order of packing your kayak?'

'The things you need first go in last.'

'Where does the first-aid kit go?'

'In the cockpit directly behind your seat where you can reach it.'

'And where do the spare matches go?'

'In the centre of your sleeping bag or bedding roll.'

This last was always considered the ultimate in canoeing wisdom.

Towards the end of the course a friend of Ian's, who lived locally, joined us for the day. He had brought along his logbook to show us the trips he'd made and the miles he'd paddled. One entry said, 'Battery Pond, wind force four.' The Battery Pond being an open-air swimming pool on the sea front!

This, too, became a catch-phrase with Archie and me. Whenever conditions looked a bit scary, one or other of us was bound to relieve the tension by shouting, 'Battery Pond, wind force four!' Certainly, it has been my experience over the years that some people who can perform all sorts of wonders and fancy strokes in a heated swimming pool cannot do them when it really counts: in the rough, cold sea, tired and in a fully laden canoe. Anyway, as far as the test was concerned, we both came up smiling.

Two weeks later, after some intensive practice, we were back again for another week's course for the Instructor's Certificate. This time we had the hallmarks of real canoeists: the hard corn in the groove between thumb and first finger where the paddle rotates in the hand, the tell-tale mark in the small of the back caused by the rear of the cockpit, the two worn patches on the outer heels of our canvas shoes, the result of paddling with feet splayed out. There were ten of us on the course. On the first day someone had to quit the course with severe sunburn. On the second day we lost another member of the group who capsized and came up unconscious. He had experienced a close encounter with a jellyfish and, unluckily, had proved to be allergic to its sting . . . On the third day a shoulder was dislocated. And now there were seven. We began to eye each other nervously like potential victims in an Agatha Christie play. On the fourth day one of our lot decided to take his own homemade fibreglass kayak out in rather blustery conditions. It had been made from a mould in two halves, the hull and the top deck being joined with strips of glass bandage and resin along the seam. Somewhere between Largs and Cumbrae Island, the two halves came apart and the kayak sank. And then there were six. In fact, the owner of the 'collapsible' canoe didn't leave the course, but simply switched to one of the kayaks provided by the SCA. The real victim was Drew who had a tough time instructing such a mad bunch.

When it was my turn to have a go at instructing the others I got them all neatly lined up in their kayaks about twenty yards off the beach while I demonstrated some stroke or other. What was so amusing about my well-planned lesson? I wondered. I soon found out. A paddle steamer was passing close behind me. Its wash carried the lot of us way up the beach, leaving us high and dry.

Drew simply couldn't get through to us that, instead of putting our heads down and paddling away like mad, we must develop the habit of continually looking around in all directions to see where everyone was, what shipping was approaching, etc. By way of making his point, he gradually dropped behind the group and then sneaked into a little bay. We were more than a mile on before anyone noticed.

I remember the visiting tester asking me, 'There is a strong onshore wind. What would you do if a member of your group capsizes close to cliffs and is in danger of being smashed to pieces on the rocks?'

'I wouldn't have got into that situation in the first place,' I replied.

I thought that was the only really responsible answer. The expected solution, however, was that you appoint the strongest paddlers in the group to use their towing lines to tow the capsized canoe and its unseated rider further out before going through the usual rescue drill.

I passed, all the same, as did Archie. Soon after that, with the help of Dave Whitelaw from Cumbernauld High School, we set up an evening class for making fibreglass kayaks. It was Dave's own design, The Tern. Mine was yellow and curving at both ends. Archie wanted to name it the *Banana*, but I named it the

Argo, after the ship in which Jason set out in search of the Golden Fleece.

'We'll be the Argonauts of the Western Isles,' I said. And so, with new kayaks and newly found skills, we were ready, at last, for the major league. Well, almost ready.

Chapter 2

Readiness is All . . . Well, Almost All

Rough water training

To feel a tingle of excitement in every nerve, to feel adrenalin pumping through the body, to feel really alive, is a marvellous experience, but fear is something different, something ugly. No passion so effectually robs the mind of all its powers of acting and reasoning as fear. And the way to combat fear is through training. Knowing that you are prepared, that you can cope with the situation even if it gets worse, that you have something in reserve, that is what dispels fear. It has always seemed to me that plenty of practice is worth any amount of bravery. Courage, unless accompanied by competence and well-founded confidence, is merely foolhardiness. In my own preparations for the major league, two things in particular needed attention. Firstly, I had never sat in a cramped cockpit for more than two and a half hours without getting out of my kayak and stretching my legs. Perhaps this was due in part to the fact that, in the comparatively sheltered waters in which I had been canoeing, land was never too far away and there was never any real need to do a longer stint than that; and partly it was because, until I made a canoe for myself with a seat moulded to the shape of my own backside, I had been in such agony from pins and needles in the legs, numb bum and 'the fidgets' that to inflict more pain than was necessary upon myself would have been taking masochism too far. Even in a car, which is spacious by comparison, two or three hours can seem a long time. I knew, however, that many of the trips to which I aspired contained crossings of five hours or more, the capacity to deal with the 'or more' being a crucial factor in survival. Supposing one arrived at the other side and found it too rough to land? Or what if an adverse wind added another two or three hours onto the time it took? So I embarked on a programme of building up the distances paddled without landing. Helensburgh to Dunoon, a quarter of an hour on the beach for lunch and home again. Then, next time I would eat my lunch in my kayak twenty yards off the beach before paddling home again. And so on, gradually increasing both the mileage and the length between the breaks ashore.

Secondly, I wanted to be able to Eskimo-roll my canoe. These days it is an ability which is commonplace, youngsters can do it a hundred times non-stop using a table tennis bat instead of a paddle, or even with their hands alone. A quarter of a century ago, however, it was still a bit of a party piece, a trick that carried a certain prestige, something that somehow always managed to crop up casually in conversation if one could actually do it. There are dozens of different ways of rolling a canoe. The one I chose to teach myself, as being one of the easiest and also one of the most reliable for a heavy sea kayak, was the pawlatta. Basically, from the upside-down position, it is a long sweep of the paddle to one side of the kayak, from front to rear, which brings you halfway up, followed by a push with the flat of the blade on the surface and a rotation of the hips. A slim sea kayak is worn like a garment fitted from the hips and a great deal of the effective control of a kayak comes from the hips.

The drawings in the book I had borrowed from the library made it look easy. But when you're upside-down, the ocean floor is where the sky used to be, everything that a few seconds ago was on your left is suddenly on your right and the top of your paddle blade has now become the underside. I spent weeks of practice in total disorientation, unable to figure out where the surface was, rolling myself further under rather than up, becoming increasingly bruised and battered by my contortions inside a kayak which seemed to be made of nothing but sharp projections and rough edges. My knees and shins were black and blue from being scraped and banged against the cockpit in countless hasty exits motivated by this unreasonable desire of mine to breathe in air rather than water.

At first I practised in shallow water about twenty yards off the end of my garden. When all else fails, the Irvine Push is a stroke to be recommended. It consists of placing one end of your paddle on the seabed and pushing yourself upright – so called because Irvine, on the Ayrshire coast, has a large area of shallow estuary and lots of cunning canoeists. I had not reckoned, however, on the kind folk of Helensburgh, who, on seeing someone thrashing and jerking about upside down in a canoe, invariably phoned the police or the local lifeboat. Tired of protesting that I didn't want to be rescued, I took to paddling across to a remote bay on the other side of the estuary, where my only audience was a somewhat amazed seal.

Finally the day arrived when I managed ten successful rolls one after the other on the right-hand side, followed by another ten in quick succession on the left-hand side.

'I can roll! I can roll!' I shouted to the seal.

'Ah, but can you do it in deep water?' his sceptical expression seemed to say.

Out in the middle of the estuary, with nobody else in sight, the water looked so black, so deep, so cold. Supposing I tried a roll and failed? What would I do then?

I dithered, fussing with my spray deck. Was this going to be the story of my rock climbing all over again? On the practice boulders, a few feet above the ground, I could make moves on almost non-existent holds. I was a human fly. But a couple of hundred feet up, the same moves became impossible, unthinkable.

'Which is it?' said the seal inside my head. 'Can you roll or can't you?'

'But it's stupid to do it so far out, on my own.

'Not if you're certain you're not going to fail.'

'But . . .'

'Well, do you have confidence in your own ability or don't you?'

'Yes, I do, I do!'

'Prove it then.'

As I completed my roll, the seal whispered to me, 'Maybe that was just a fluke. If you really believed in yourself you'd do it again.'

The next step was to be able to roll in rough, breaking water. One of the difficulties of this is that once the surface ceases to be flat and still, it is much harder to gauge where it is from the upside-down position. On one occasion, when the water was murky with churned up sediment, I became completely disorientated and unable to find the surface. I lost all sense of which way was up and which was down. I was running out of breath. What should I do? If I came out of the canoe how would I get back in again? Calm yourself, you're getting it wrong because you're panicking. I relaxed and as soon as I did so I could feel my paddle, of its own accord, solving the problem for me by naturally floating to the surface. On another occasion, I did a deliberate capsize amongst breaking surf and struck my head on a hidden boulder. I hung upside-down in a daze. There must be some mechanism in the brain which automatically closes down the breathing in situations like this. I only know that, without being aware of it, I didn't try to breathe. I brought myself upright again, not by any conscious action, but because the drill was ingrained and automatic. After that, I always carried a crash helmet with me – the kind that lets water drain out of it – and put it on when going through surf or when I couldn't tell what lay below the surface. I suppose what I should also have done was to stop going out on my own. But, with the sea lapping at the garden wall, whispering, calling to me . . .

Throughout the winter I practised in the school swimming pool. I practised remaining upside-down for a count of twenty before rolling up; I practised throwing my paddle away and, still inside my kayak, swimming to it and then rolling up; I practised coming out of the canoe, getting back into it again while it was upside down and rolling up. Then, with the approach of summer, I did it all over again in the rough, cold sea. And I discovered a minor irony along the way – that, once you can roll a sea kayak, your chances of having to do so in earnest are considerably reduced. In learning to Eskimo-roll you gain such mastery of the basic recovery strokes and control over the kayak that an involuntary capsize becomes an increasingly rare event. The very fact that you know you can do it gives you confidence. A relaxed and confident paddler is far more likely to remain the right way up than someone who is anxious and tense and does not have the confidence simply to let well-trained reflexes cope with things instinctively. When the going gets difficult, the best advice I can give to a companion – and the hardest to take – is, 'Relax. Believe in the kayak and in yourself.'

About 200 yards from my house is a sea wall some twelve feet in height, above which is a promenade. When the tide is up and the wind blowing from a westerly direction, the waves crash against the wall and bounce back into the next rank of oncoming waves. This collision of waves, which is called clapotis, creates an area of steep, jumbled and chaotic water. 'The wall run' provided invaluable practice, simulating as it did the kind of seas I would encounter beneath sea cliffs or wherever two bodies of moving water warred with each other. Within sight of old ladies taking their Sunday constitutional and exercising their dogs, I prepared myself, in controlled conditions from which I could safely extract myself, for the real thing. And that is one of the fascinations of activities like mountaineering or sea kayaking: they are more than games with made-up rules and a referee to see fair play or stop the fight if it gets too one-sided; there is no pretence, the dangers are real and the penalty for failure is not to have a free kick awarded against you, or to count to one hundred before you can join in again. The 'rules' are the laws of nature, and the forfeit may be your life. People talk about challenging the elements, about pitting themselves against the forces of nature. Nothing can quite compare with that experience (well, almost nothing) – as long as you're fairly certain you're going to win. A little *frisson* of doubt, perhaps, but no more. Fear is not enjoyable, and dying, in nine cases out of ten, is not heroism but the result of inadequate training and preparation, bad planning and poor judgement. (Well, almost always: luck also has something to do with it.) Before I start wagging the finger or sounding too smug I'd better confess that only good luck has saved me from several mishaps. Anyway, to return to the old ladies on the promenade, they came to know me quite well and would even wave and hold up their dogs to get a better look at the merman with his wooden flippers who splashed up and down the length of the wall, for some strange reason, always in the roughest bit of water.

Progression by easy steps is a basic maxim for learning anything. It is certainly true of sea kayaking. Someone who has never sat in a canoe, on reading about one of the expeditions I describe in this book, might think, 'My goodness, I could never do that, I'd be absolutely terrified!' And so would I be if I was pitched straight into it instead of slowly building up to it. When you know you can handle the situation because you've met it before and managed it successfully, instead of being frightening, it is exhilarating. Of course, being able to look out of my study window and keep an eye on what the waves were doing made it a lot easier to plan these easy steps towards confidence and to venture out only when things were just a little bit harder than they had been the last time, so that I always knew (well, almost always) that my skill was equal to the task.

Readiness for the real thing also means having access to essential information and the ability to interpret it correctly. I am constantly struck by the deceptively innocent and clear blue countenance of the sea on Ordnance Survey maps when compared with the same stretch of water on an Admiralty chart, black with symbols and warnings of wrecks, underwater cables, submerged reefs, rip tides, eddies and prohibited areas. I have to admit, though, that I want advice, foreknowledge and forewarning only up to a certain point. On some Alpine mountain routes, you can follow painted red arrows all the way to the top. I hope the day never comes when the *West Coast Pilot* and other guides are so detailed, and the weather forecasts so accurate, that nothing at all remains to chance. For me at least, there has to be an element of exploration, of venturing into the unknown.

I am often asked how I manage to do a demanding full-time job, to research and write novels as well as find the time and energy not only to go mountaineering and sea kayaking, but also to practise and keep fit for these physical activities. There are various answers. In, the first place, mountaineering and sea kayaking are not in competition with the other things I do with my time or my energy, they are mutually supporting. Contact with the hills and the sea and the natural environment recharges my batteries and makes me more efficient and productive at the desk-work, better able to cope with the stress, not less able. Similarly, the mental work and the indoor work sharpen my appetite for the great outdoors and make the contrast all the more enjoyable. I worked for several months, once, with the Forestry Commission in Scotland, clearing land of bracken, digging drainage ditches, hammering in fencing posts, planting trees (the one thing I didn't do was what I had imagined forestry people did all the time: chop down trees), and by the weekend I was cured of all desire for any more fresh air.

Another solution, for me, is to combine two activities at once. For example, I watch television whilst pedalling my exercise bicycle. Before going to Bogota to research into the lives of the street kids for my book *Fallen Angels,* I learnt much of my Spanish with a cassette and headphones whilst either pedalling or paddling. Shouting out Spanish phrases in an excruciatingly bad accent is less embarrassing in an empty expanse of sea than elsewhere. I've even been known to burst into song in these circumstances. When I'm on my own in my kayak, usually doing a training stint, I am quite often writing my current book at the same time, composing the dialogues and paragraphs in my head, then briefly stopping in mid-water to jot it all down before I forget. I can never read any of my own books without the places where I wrote certain bits being recalled vividly. For example, in *Lord of the Dance,* the scene at the riverside with Bamian the dwarf and the guru instantly brings to mind a blustery day down Loch Long; the first encounter with the leper woman was written while I sat naked on an exposed sandbar in the middle of the Clyde, trying to get it all down before a rising tide engulfed me and floated my kayak away. At first, I wrote on rigid plastic squares, cut out from the sides of plastic containers. Then I discovered that yacht chandlers actually sold waterproof note-books with plastic pages, which can be wiped clean and used again. On one occasion, the words were flowing particularly well and I completely filled my notebook. There's this panicky feeling writers get that, if they don't immediately get their creative gems down in writing, the words will evaporate, slip away, never again to be remembered in quite the same brilliant form. So, with my indelible felt pen, I scrawled feverishly on the fibreglass deck of my kayak. And, when I had filled up the deck as far as I could reach forward from the cockpit, I wrote along the side of the hull. On reaching home in my floating masterpiece, I pulled my kayak into my untidy, weed-infested garden and quickly jotted it all down into a notebook and thence onto the typewriter. 'Fluid prose,' one critic said later, when reviewing the book. And why do I mention my untidy garden? To make the point that there is no such thing as not having time, only of having different priori-ties . . . a point upon which, in general, men sit more comfortably than women.

These training outings of which I have written are also a time for photography. On expeditions the kayak is too fully packed to allow room for my big Mamiya camera which takes large-format 120-size film. Although my pocket-size waterproofed (and capa-ble of floating) Minolta is ideal for these expeditions, it doesn't quite give me the size of negative I want for quality enlargements or for working in my darkroom, 'blowing up' some corner of a picture that particularly takes my fancy. There are certain places which I visit again and again, always hoping for that elusive perfect picture – the sun glinting on the rippled, textured mud flats, briefly exposed at low tide; the underside of the abandoned Craigendoran Pier with lights hafting through gaps in the planking above, or bouncing of the waves sluicing between the uprights, dappling the time-worn timbers; the rocks on the Kilcregganshore, sculptures by Henry Moore or Barbara Hepworth, smooth and rounded like a woman's body, sometimes light and dusty, reminiscent of the down on the small of a back or the nape of a neck, sometimes gleaming dark and wet. And then there is my adopted tree stump. It lies in a bay in the tidal zone, scoured smooth and bleached to a fine-grained silver white, contrasting with the dark seaweed which clings to it. Within its upturned and barnacle-encrusted root-system dark pools harbour tiny shells of perfect symmetry. Yes, for me, the sea and the tidal zones around its edges will always be one of my priorities.

Chapter 3

The Best Part of a Goodish Bit

Belnahua, Scarba and the Garvellachs

Archie's green Riley nosed out of the line of cars and, in one thundering surge up the long hill, passed the lot.

'Not bad, considering we've got two kayaks on the roof!' I said.

We were heading for Easdale on the island of Seil which is joined to the mainland by Clachan Bridge, 'the bridge over the Atlantic', so called because it crosses all of twenty feet of the Atlantic in the form of the narrow Clachan Sound. Easdale was our launching point for the islands of Belnahua, Scarba, the Garvellachs and after that . . . after that we might topple off the edge of the world. It was our first big trip, our entry into the major league.

Near the top of the long hill the Riley coughed once or twice, lost power and glided to a halt.

'Nae petrol,' Archie said.

Archie knew the road well and realised that, once we topped the rise, we could freewheel the mile to the next petrol station. We were pushing the heavy brute up the hill when an American couple stopped for us.

'Out of gas?' the man enquired. 'Wanna syphon some from our tank?'

Archie was seized by some irresistible urge to play up to all those silly stories about mean Scotsmen. Politely declining the generous offer he declared that our tank was full and that we were pushing the car purely for reasons of economy. We were so helpless with laughter at this brilliant piece of wit that we very nearly let the Riley roll all the way back down the slope.

Just before midday we reached Seil Island, stopping briefly for a drink at the inn called 'Tigh an Truish', the House of Trousers, so called because, when the wearing of the kilt was banned after the failure of the Jacobite rebellion, the local people would stop here to change into trousers before crossing to the mainland. A man at the next table was telling a yarn about duck-eating pikes that would seize their prey by the legs and drag them under.

'Would a pike eat an entire duck?' I asked.

He stroked his chin; 'Mmm, the best part of a goodish bit.'

Easdale lay spread below us. Beyond it the sea was a charge of kicking white horses. 'Force four, gusting to five' the weather forecast on the radio had said. It seemed more than that. Force five in the Clyde Estuary had been manageable, but in an expanse of water open to the Atlantic it was altogether more menacing. We reflected on our hitherto sheltered lives and said nothing. Parking next to a quayside cafe, we went in for a bite to eat. The waitress glanced out of the window and eyed our two kayaks shuddering in the wind on top of the Riley.

'You'll not be going out today,' she said. It was a statement, not a question.

Archie and I exchanged glances.

'We're thinking of going out to Belnahua,' I said.

She stomped off, shaking her head. She clearly thought we were mad.

Returning with our two plates of eggs and chips, she thumped them down in front of us.

'That's the last meal you'll ever eat!'

'The condemned man ate a hearty breakfast,' Archie observed and we laughed uneasily.

Beyond the harbour wall the waves seemed enormous. A mile out, a freighter bashed through heavy seas, plumes of spray rising from the iron cliffs of its hull.

'When you're in something as small as a kayak, the waves don't smash into you,' we told the waitress more than once.

'You see, a kayak is so light it rises over even the biggest waves like a cork.'

She sniffed. 'So you've said . . . several times.'

Archie drew lines through a puddle of spilt tea, turning the formica table-top into a map of the Firth of Lorn, marking in the rip tides and eddies, streaming like banners off the islands all around. Two little tea leaves represented us. The four miles out to Belnahua hadn't looked very far on the chart – but on a chart you don't see the vast swell rolling in from the Atlantic. For several evenings, fortified by cups of coffee, we had planned the trip. Between us we had assembled and consulted a variety of sources: the Admiralty chart for the area, the *West Coast Pilot*, *Clyde Cruising Club Sailing Directions*, *Pocket Tidal Stream Atlas*, and the tidal prediction tables for the current year. For our purposes, *Clyde Cruising Club Sailing Directions* was the most helpful because it has the needs and concerns of smaller boats in mind, whereas the *West Coast Pilot* is for bigger ships. Of Scarba Sound, the former says: 'A strong tide runs through this sound, from three knots at Ardluing to seven knots at Pladda, or Fladda as it is called on some charts. The tide makes 1 hr. before H.W. or L.W.'

Since we would be travelling the length of the sound from Belnahua at its north end to Scarba at the southern end, we pondered the significance of this paragraph. Our normal paddling speed was about four or five knots and, going flat out, we could manage six knots for short periods. So if the tidal current at Fladda was running at seven knots, there was no way we could paddle against it. We would have to make sure that we were always going in the same direction as the current – that is to say, southwards on the ebb tide and northwards on the flood tide . . .

Not that it was quite as straightforward as simply using the tidal prediction tables to calculate when this would be, because 'the tide makes 1 hr. before H.W. or L.W.'. This phenomenon is mentioned again in a subsequent paragraph: 'The flood and ebb turn 1 hr. before H.W. and L.W. in the middle of the sound, but close to the Lunga side the ebb runs till almost low water.' That the tide would be doing different things in different parts of the sound came as no surprise. Whereas the flood tide (incoming high tide) flows north through the sound, wherever it meets a gap between islands it pours westwards out to sea; and just to mystify the poor navigator even more, further south, off the Kintyre Peninsula, it flows south, and further north, as it comes round the top end of Skye, the tidal stream is moving eastwards. No wonder navigation is referred to as 'the Black Art'!

Crump! Exploding fragments of white leapt the harbour wall. The waitress threw us a pitying glance and, with a quick stroke of her sponge, wiped us out.

We lifted the kayaks off the roof-rack and began packing them for the trip, trying to cram in tent, stove, food, sleeping bags, fuel, spare clothes . . . A knot of people had gathered to watch us.

'Aren't they the kind that tip over?' someone asked.

Crump! I could feel the stones vibrate. We put on our neoprene wet-suits, something we hadn't normally done up till then unless we were deliberately capsizing to practise rescues and rolls. Before, we had found them too constricting for a long paddle, too hot and sticky. Now we found them reassuring.

'Hey, mister! Can I have a shot in your boat?' a small boy asked me.

A dog sniffed at the stern of Archie's kayak and threatened to lift its leg.

'Stick to the sea!' Archie said. 'It's safer! Come on, let's go!'

We carried our kayaks to the water's edge in silence. Inside the harbour's protecting arm we glided past rows of moored boats, not seeing them, seeing only the waves beyond the exit, sizing them up.

'Battery Pond, force four!' Archie shouted as if it were a battle cry and launched himself at the waves.

I braced my knees against the inside of the hull, gripped the paddle a little harder and drove my bows at the open sea. Chunky, heaving waters bounced at me from every angle. I punched through them, dominating them, imposing my own speed and direction on them.

Beyond the zone of turbulent encounter an immence ocean swell rolled in from the Atlantic. We paddled up long green slopes down which smaller waves were running. With each approaching wave the horizon tilted upwards. After about twenty minutes, the sight of waves as big as hills sweeping towards me ceased to be frightening. Occasionally, the smaller waves on the big flanks of these monsters were breaking, but the big ones themselves bore no malice. When Archie was in a different trough from me he disappeared from sight, then he would rise into view again, grinning from ear to ear. I realised I was grinning too. We were actually enjoying it! In almost any other type of vessel I would have been feeling seasick. All those years I had been sailing with my father, I had felt sick nearly every time we went out. Whether it was the absence of the smells with which I associate feeling sick – engine-oil, paint, old rope – or the fact that my mind and body were fully occupied with no time to dwell on the dreaded malady, I don't know, but I, who was once sick before the ferry from Dover had even cast off, have never been sick in a canoe. Height above water level may also have something to do with it. You have only to observe how much more the top of a mast swings from side to side in a swell compared to the hull, to know what I mean. The bigger the vessel, the more the sea is something alien and apart, the more its natural rhythms are transformed into unnatural pitching and rolling. Rising into view then sinking again was the silhouette of Belnahua and of the lighthouse on Fladda; beyond that the dark outline of the Garvellachs, strung across the horizon; to our right the cliffs of Mull, their base flecked white with soundless breakers; to our left the long corridor with the mainland on one side and Lunga, Scarba and Jura on the other, the inner passageway of the western seaboard.

Our kayaks grounded on Belnahua's black slate sand. I stood on the beach while it heaved up and down, emulating the motion of the sea. This was our first real island, our first taste of leaving the mainland behind and 'getting away from it all'. I had imagined that islands such as this would be havens of peace and quiet. I was mistaken. The noise from the thousands of gulls as they wheeled and dived and made their shrill protests was almost deafening. Archie and I had to shout at each other to make ourselves heard. We carried our kayaks over black, rounded boulders to where the grass began. Before exploring the island – you can walk right round it in about fifteen minutes – we decided to take off our wet-suits. Unfortunately Archie's zip jammed. While he struggled with it, we fantasised about what it would be like if he was stuck in it for several months. Would his skin go corpse-white and crinkly like it does when it's covered by a plaster? From there we progressed to a modern version of one of the *Just So* stories, entitled 'Archie the Irritable', based on the one about how the rhinoceros took his hide off and, while he was having a swim, someone rubbed crumbs into it, which for ever after made him itchy and short-tempered.

'Well, never mind, Archie. If you can't get out of it, I expect some seal will love you, even if Betty won't.'

We stood there, still in our wet-suits, savouring the freedom, the feeling of having left our cares and our work-day masks behind, of being born again. Round a headland and into the bay chugged a small fishing boat, piled with lobster pots. The salty, unshaven character who landed from it took one look at us and said, 'You'll be teachers, then?'

Somewhat deflated, we agreed we were.

'I used to be one, too,' he said. 'I packed it in. Man, it was the smell of those school dinners!'

We chatted, took a nip from a whisky bottle in his pocket and allowed him the honour of unzipping Archie before he chugged out of the bay again.

'How could he tell?'

'It was the way you carried your paddle like a tawse.'
'It was not! It was you shouting at the gulls to line up!'

It was late afternoon and time for our tour of inspection round the island. Belnahua was formerly a slate quarrying island. Slates from Belnahua and other quarries in this area were carried by the puffers up and down the west coast of Scotland. Large parts of Glasgow are still roofed by Belnahua slates. However, with the advent of cheaper and lighter roofing materials, the slate quarrying industry fell into decline. Belnahua had been almost completely worked out anyway. The centre of the island, at one time a low hill, is now a huge cavity, filled with brackish water which has seeped through from the sea. Around its black edges, relics of a bygone age rust in the salt air: a winch, an old boiler, and unidentified bits of machinery weeping red tears, gradually flaking into extinction. On the southern side of this dismal lake is the ghost village of Belnahua. Roofless houses, filled with tumbled stones and nettles. As we moved nearer to the shore the noise of the gulls reached new peaks of frenzied screaming. Glancing down, I saw a gull chick at my feet, immobile amongst the pebbles. And there was another, keeping absolutely still in its little declivity. We trod carefully, but the outraged parent gulls were not appeased.

The sun set behind a fleet of anchored islands, turning the sea to molten gold and crimson; and in its afterglow were greens, pale yellows and fires of red. We slept in the main street of the village, a red light from the Fladda Lighthouse penetrating the fabric of our tent. Three flashes . . . an eighteen-second gap, then another three flashes. The gulls were still wide awake, the sea was shouting with many voices . . . or was it the villagers abroad at night? Flash, flash, flash . . . eighteen seconds . . . flash, flash . . . it was more effective than counting sheep.

We were up early next morning to hear the shipping forecast on my pocket radio – force four, south westerly – and to make sure we caught the ebb tide going south through Scarba Sound.

But first we wanted to visit Fladda. The lighthouse is no longer manned and has been reduced to the status of an automatic beacon. The whitewashed keeper's house was still there, though, and the whitewashed garden wall, inside which thrived rare and exotic plants – at least, I thought they were, until I realised they were garden vegetables, cabbages in stages of development never seen when they are grown to be eaten, potatoes returning to the wild, rhubarb in flower. The beach by the jetty was a billion tiny shells, recently wetted by the turning tide, more delicate even than the smallest finger-nail of a newborn babe, more subtle even in their shades of pink and yellow than last night's sunset. I filled a jar with them. Later, I tried, not very successfully, to identify them from various reference books. Some, I think, are of the periwinkle type, others may belong to the Tellinidae family. No matter what they're called, in the years since then, hardly a day goes by but their beauty gives me pleasure.

Scarba Sound was sheltered from the westerly wind and the swell, otherwise all hell would have been let loose as those forces encountered and did battle with the seven-knot ebb tide. We sat there, hardly bothering to paddle as the shores whizzed by. Glassy upwellings or miniature whirlpools would suddenly whip my bows through forty degrees or more, rippling cross-currents within the main stream would whisk me yards off course in a matter of seconds. We pulled over to the Scarba side. On the exposed rocks close to the shore seals and their fat little pups were basking. The seals in the Firth of Lorn and the inner waters are the common seal, not to be confused with the Atlantic or grey seal which is found off the outer isles. The common seal breeds during late summer. There is a delayed implantation until some time between November and January, and the pups are born in June. Because they can go to sea almost at once and be suckled there, they are much less open to accident than are the pups of the grey seal. Despite our silent approach, we never got nearer than about twenty or thirty feet before they raised their heads and slithered down the rock, hitting the water with a splash.

The ebb delivered us to the south-east corner of Scarba, some six miles from Fladda, in well under an hour. We climbed a hill and sat watching the volumes of water squirting eastwards through the Corryvreckan, the strait between Scarba and Jura. This was the tide-race on the ebb tide, which is gentle compared with the westerly tide-race on the flood, when the notorious whirlpool develops. Even so, we were awed by its power. We climbed higher, taking a diagonal route up an east-facing heather slope. Rounding a spur, we came across a herd of fifty or more red deer. At that time, the owner of Scarba did not permit the shooting of deer and their numbers were increasing. The true home of red deer is dense woodland. With the deforestation of the Scottish highlands and islands through felling, fire and grazing by sheep, the red deer adapted to moorland feeding. In Europe, where the red deer inhabit forests and can enjoy richer browsing, they can weigh up to forty stone. On the Scottish moor, however, they seldom weigh more than fifteen stone. I am told that the deer sometimes swim from one island to another. How many drown in the Corryvreckan I shudder to think. Perhaps, like us, they consult their tidal tables before making a move. A browsing head jerked up in alarm, then another and another. The herd broke into a trot and, wheeling in unison, disappeared over the brow of the hill.

Lunch was soup in a flask, sandwiches and a spread of land and water, islands, ocean and sea lochs wrapped in the blue haze of a sunny June day. There was no hurry. Slack water was still three hours away. Our plan was to retrace our route as far as the Grey Dog, the passage between the north end of Scarba and Lunga. This was our gateway to the Garvellach Isles. The Grey Dog, although shorter in length, is every bit as fierce as the Corryvreckan. The only sensible time for us to attempt it was at the period of slack water which would occur at the turn of the tide. We sunbathed and took photographs and slowly wended our way back to the kayaks. On the way I picked up a cast antler. It had three tines on it, indicating that the stag was five years old when it cast this particular antler. The antlers are cast between February and April, the young stags casting theirs later than the older ones who have more tines to grow each year. During the second year of life a stag develops a pair of simple unbranched stems. In the third year the new antlers bear a tine or side-branch and an extra tine is added each succeeding year when the new antlers are grown. After the third tine the antler spreads into three top branches. When a pair of antlers totals twelve points, the stag is known as a royal.

Things were brewing beneath us as we slipped through the Grey Dog. Emerging at the far end, we turned and looked back. The entire body of water in the strait was tilting upwards, the stronger tidal stream at its eastern end causing the sea to pile up till its level was some ten feet higher than where we were. Within minutes it would be roaring through the gap, trying to even itself out. We remembered a pressing engagement on the uninhabited Garvellachs and paddled off at high speed.

The swell on the exposed Atlantic side of Scarba was bigger than anything we had experienced yesterday, and yet there was no menace in its immensity. It was like the deep, slow breathing of some vast slumbering beast; it was like being in a dream about a magical undulating landscape; it was how a bird must feel soaring up and up on a thermal. And so to the Garvellachs, or, to give them their Gaelic name, Hinba (pronounced Eenba), the Isles of the Sea: four small islands in line astern. The largest and south most of these, Eileach an Naoimh, was where we planned to camp for the night.

Part of our plan for the trip was to supplement our food with what we could catch or collect. Not so much because there wasn't enough room in our kayaks for several days' supplies, but simply for the fun of it. With this in mind, we attached our nylon lines to cleats on the stern deck and trailed spinners behind us – little twirling, twinkling metal fish with a hook on the end. I have often caught mackerel this way. Out here we were hoping for something bigger. Soon my line began to jerk. I was definitely paddling against something that was pulling hard in the opposite direction. I put my hand on the line. Vibrating energy surged up it. I began to wind it in, my kayak moving backwards and leaning at an alarming angle. Archie rafted up beside me to give me stability. Slowly the tugging, fighting catch came to the surface and was flopping and jerking on the lap of my spray deck. I tried to hold the fish still while Archie clubbed it with the blade of his paddle. It took longer than we liked. It was just over two feet long. From the power and strength of it I had expected something bigger on the end of the line. It was a sobering thought that I probably couldn't have handled it on my own and it might even have had me over. We argued about whether it was a big sea trout or a medium-sized salmon. They are of the same family and have much the same bodies, gills and mouths, but trout are less silvery, more of a grey-greenish hue and have more spots.

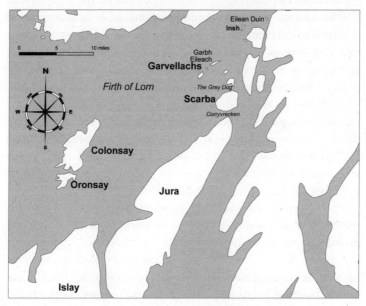

The Garvellachs, Scarba and surrounding islands

'Which do you want it to be?' Archie asked.

'I think it would taste nicer if it was a salmon.'

'Right! A salmon it is then.'

With our catch safely, if rather uncomfortably, stowed between my legs, we headed for Eileach an Naoimh.

The earliest stone buildings to survive in Scotland from the Christian era are on Eileach an Naoimh, built in the ninth century on the site of the little wooden monastery founded in the sixth century in the name of St Brendan. St Columba of Iona used the Hinba monastery as a 'desert' or retreat. When Brendan sailed from Ireland, at the age of almost ninety, to visit Columba, he found him on Eileach an Naoimh. We landed on the island and erected our tent near the ruins, close to the beehive-shaped constructions which were used as cells by the monks and solitaries of the Celtic Church.

The salmon, wrapped in tinfoil and braised in its own juices in the embers of a driftwood fire, was one of the most delicious things I have ever eaten. This was accompanied by mussels collected off the beach and stewed in tinned milk, and freshly picked young nettles, lightly steamed. The latter tastes very like spinach. While we ate, I told Archie the story of how I had been canoeing once with a group which included an attractive young woman. It was a very hot day and we were all paddling in nothing but swimming suits or trunks. During a brief rest I asked her to rub sun tan oil on my back.

'What wonderful muscles!' she exclaimed.

'Oh, do you really think so?' I replied, as pleased as Punch.

'Yes, look at them over there on the rocks, what a meal they'd make!'

In June, in these latitudes, there is daylight till ten or eleven in the evening, so we had plenty of time for some leisurely exploration. We decided to cruise gently in our kayaks up part of the four-mile chain of islands, keeping to the eastern side because, on the steep western side, the enormous swell would be hurling itself against cliffs. Between islands a window opened onto wider vistas. But more than that, in these shallow straits we were in the ephemeral world of the half-flood tide, a world which exists for only a few hours each day when the tide has yet to rise for another three or four hours. It is a world of intriguingly narrow channels imperceptibly swelling, of a half-revealed underworld, of short-lived lagoons, and forests of exposed seaweed, gently swaying. Drifting over a chalice brimming with emerald-green water, watching my own zeppelin shadow flitting across the seabed, I became aware of an otter feeding on the shore. Intent upon devouring an eel, it paid no heed to our silent, gliding approach. We watched it for several minutes before backing quietly away, leaving it still clutching its meal between its webbed front paws. Returning to Eileach an Naoimh, we clambered through lush, dense, untamed vegetation to the highest point. Marvelling at the rare quality of light that seems unique to the western isles, we lingered, absorbing the view towards the Hebrides and the setting sun. There is something very special about the Garvellachs, the Isles of the Sea. They emanate the same feeling of spirituality that many people have felt about Iona. I am not sure what it is, but both Archie and I remarked on it. It has to be more than the simple fact that both Iona and the Garvellachs are small, peaceful islands. Recently, my wife and I have begun regular sessions of meditation. Our elder daughter, who has been practising meditation much longer, visited us and said, 'I knew you'd taken up meditation as soon as I entered the house. You can always tell. There is an atmosphere of calmness and tranquillity in a house where people meditate.'

Does the influence of those monks reach out to us across eleven centuries or more? Or could it be that those early saints chose these two islands because they sensed other forces already there?

That should have been the end of a perfect day ... but it wasn't. The breeze dropped and the midges came out in force. (No, they are not the 'other forces' to which I referred!) They attacked us in dark, voracious clouds. They filled the tent; the walls, the roof, the very air was black with them. They made life a misery and a torment until we could stand it no longer. Hastily pulling down the tent, we flung our belongings into the kayaks and paddled like madmen away from the island. We kept paddling through the long twilight known as the *simer dim* until we reached Belnahua, a place which had the inestimable merit of being open to the winds, blessed, midge-dispelling winds.

In the middle of the night a storm blew up. Next morning the storm continued unabated. It was magnificent to watch . . . from the safety of land – and we intended to keep it that way. Belnahua may not have midges, but it didn't have fresh water either. The water in the excavated hole in the middle of the island was brackish and undrinkable. We used the last drops from our plastic water container for a breakfast cup of tea. After searching the island we found one pool of rain water, green and stagnant and foul smelling.

'No way are we going to drink that! No way!' we declared.

On the second day, we were still trapped on the island, the storm showing no signs of letting up. We took another look at the pool. This time it seemed a little less foul, but definitely not drinkable. The storm continued into the third day. The water in the pool was quite inviting now, almost drinkable . . . almost. Dehydrated, desperate for liquid, we considered ways of purifying the water by boiling it and straining it through cloth; we considered killing the gull chicks and sucking their blood. Finally we opted for braving the storm and making the crossing to the mainland. If we had been nervous about the crossing from Easdale to Belnahua, the prospect of the return was terrifying. The waves were no bigger than before, but they were steeper and faster, with frothing crests. And it was a running sea, that is to say, we would be paddling with the waves bearing down on us from behind, the most difficult kind of sea of all to deal with. We packed the canoes without exchanging a word, the roar of the sea loud in our ears. 'Relax, relax!' I kept saying to myself, but every time a wave loomed over my shoulder, foaming and curling, I tensed; every time I rode one of the snarling tigers, teetering on its crest, I tensed; every time one swept on past me and I could watch its awesome speed and size as it careered onwards, I tensed. Archie's face rose from a trough, white and strained. Then he grinned and I grinned back. I said something reassuring and almost believed it myself. And soon after that, I thought, 'We're coping, we can do it!' And I did relax, and it became easier.

Inside Easdale harbour, we rested on our paddles. Crump! A wave exploded against the protecting wall.

Archie said, 'Well, I'd say we've done the best part of a good-ish bit. Not bad for our first real trip.'

'The first of many,' I replied. 'Once you've tasted the real thing, nothing else will do, will it?'

Archie laughed. 'Talking of tasting the real thing, I'll have a pint of lager, and after that, another one.'

Chapter 4

A Depe Holepoole

Helensburgh to Colonsay and the Corryvreckan

A major trip, starting and ending at the bottom of my garden – there was a neatness and freedom and self-sufficiency about it that was appealing. Helensburgh to Colonsay and back via the Crinan Canal and the Corryvreckan, a total round trip of about 180 miles. In all those miles one stretch, barely two miles long, occupied our thoughts more than any other. When we talked about the trip, we referred to it as the Colonsay trip, but uppermost in our minds, waking and dreaming, was the notorious strait between Jura and Scarba, the Corryvreckan. But, first, we wanted to strengthen our team. The crossing to the mainland from Belnahua, on our first big trip, had convinced Archie and me that three was a much safer number than two. Rolling a kayak in very high seas is not easy and two people can rescue a third companion in the water much more quickly and easily than can one person on his own. We were on the lookout for a suitable, like-minded companion. Then, one day, when doing a training paddle round the Cumbrae Isles, we found Martin. Or, to be exact, we found an empty kayak floating about twenty yards off a beach on Little Cumbrae. In it was a complete set of canoeing clothes, including a T-shirt on the front of which were the words 'Gobi Desert Canoe Club'. As we towed the kayak ashore we scanned the beach in vain for some sign of its owner.

From behind a boulder a man's voice said, 'Are you girls or fellows?'

'What do you mean, girls or fellows? Can't you tell the difference?'

'Not without my specs and they're in the canoe.' He stepped out from the boulder, completely naked.

'I was taking a swim, you see, and forgot the tide was coming in and . . .'

'Yeah, we know. Our kayaks have nearly floated away dozens of times.'

The three of us paddled back to Largs together. Martin was a few years younger than Archie and me and, with his sandy hair and fair eyelashes, looked even younger. He confessed to us that, on his honeymoon, the barman had been convinced he was under the legal age and had refused to serve him a drink. Martin was a little less practised than we were (at canoeing, I mean), but it was obvious from the start that he was a natural athlete and a fast learner. He lived in the same area as us, didn't have anyone else to canoe with, and followed the same sea kayakers' code:

> Leave nothing but footprints
> Take nothing but memories
> Shoot nothing but pictures.

Over a pint of beer we invited Martin to become the third member of the team, to become one of the Argonauts of the Western Isles.

Before we were put to the test as a team, before we trusted our lives to each other, we needed to get to know each other's strengths and weaknesses. We did a number of day outings together, during which we practised the deep-sea rescue drills in all the possible combinations . . . me in the water with Martin and Archie rescuing me, Archie in the water with Martin and I doing the business etc. Martin also needed initiation into the Black Art. It came as a shock to the poor innocent, for example, to learn that, whereas winds are given directional labels according to where they *come from,* tides, currents, etc, are labelled according to where they *are going*. Thus, a westerly wind is blowing from the west towards the east, but a westerly current is running in an east-west direction. Within a few weeks we were ready, and the Colonsay trip was on . . . As far as the Corryvreckan, at least. What happened then, we'd have to wait and see.

The first day and a half of a fine, settled spell of weather in July took us to Ardrishaig and the eastern entrance to the nine-mile Crinan Canal. To my mind, this was where the trip really started. The journey up to this point had been in waters we knew fairly well, being the area in which Archie and I had put in our scheduled 100 miles of paddling before the end of May. Going through the picturesque Kyles of Bute was worthy of an entry in the diary, particularly the woods which can be seen soon after passing Strone Point on the mainland, which have been so planted as to show the positions of the opposing armies at the battle of Waterloo. There is also the rather unusual phenomenon of a buoyage system which suddenly reverses itself. If a channel is marked by a buoy whose shape and colour indicate it should be kept to starboard, it means your starboard as you go upstream (in the case of a river), or in the same direction as the flood tide (in the case of tidal waters). The flood tide runs round the Isle of Bute in a clockwise direction, up the west Kyle and southwards down the east Kyle. Thus, there is a point, at the north end of the island where the two Kyles meet, where upstream becomes downstream and the buoyage system reverses (more of the Black Art!).

Also into the diary went the sighting of a school of basking sharks, playing on the surface near the entrance to Loch Fyne. There must have been about six or seven of them, some about thirty feet long. There is only one bigger fish in the sea and that is the whale shark of the Indian and Pacific oceans. I am told that baskers are quite harmless, feeding on plankton sieved through gill-rakers. However, the thought of what even a playful flip from one of those powerful tails could do to our flimsy kayaks kept us at a respectful distance from them. Baskers still come into the Firth of Clyde in July, though in much smaller numbers than in former years, owing to the fact that they were much hunted for their livers which can yield a ton of oil. Baskers were not the only fish that used to visit these parts in greater numbers. Alastair Dunnett, one autumn in the 1930s, with Seamus Adams made a canoe trip from Bowling on the Clyde to Kyle of Lochalsh and wrote a book about it called *It's Too Late in the Quest by Canoe*. A later edition of the book was given the title *It's Too Late in the Year* because that was the warning they repeatedly received throughout their journey. Anyway, in his book, he describes how, in the years 1912–1914, herring teemed in millions in these waters as far up as Inveraray on Loch Fyne. By this time, however, the inland coastal fishermen had been put out of business. Alastair Dunnett writes:

> From Fife and Ayrshire and further afield came the modern boats in hundreds, scooping up the treasure and turning it to gold. On the shore, straightening their backs from the stone-breaking at the quarries and the roadsides, the remnants of the best coastal fishermen and seamen in the world – boatless, netless, and grounded – watched them do it.

At midday on the second day of our journey, Archie, Martin and I entered the Crinan Canal. Construction of the canal began in 1794 and was completed in 1809, making it the shortest route from the Clyde to the western isles and saving eighty-five miles on the route round the Mull of Kintyre. It is little used today by the cargo puffers, fishing boats and other coastal shipping for which it was intended. However, over 2,000 yachts and leisure craft a year pass through it. The first few miles were idyllic – swans gliding gracefully beside us, grassy banks clustered with primroses and wild strawberries. Then we came to the mid way and highest point at Cairnbaan, with its series of nine locks. Bigger boats, of course, would have to work the lock gates and wait for the water levels to equalise. Our plan was simply to lift the kayaks out and portage round a lock gate every time we came to one, unless we met up with a yacht in the process of going through and we could tag on behind. What we hadn't reckoned on was the steepness and height of the banks in this part of the canal, or the weight of our fully loaded kayaks. The hoped for free ride in the wake of a yacht never materialised and, by the time we had negotiated all nine locks, we were exhausted.

Revived by a swim in the canal, we pressed on. This stretch I had visited before with Tommy Kearins when writing an article about him. Tommy, now in his fifties, had played 'the wee boy', in the Ealing comedy *The Maggie*, a film about the captain and crew of an old puffer. The film was made in 1953, but has appeared regularly on television in the years since then. Several scenes from the film were shot in this stretch of the canal, in Crinan itself and in nearby waters. The part of the puffer *Maggie* was, in fact, played by two working puffers, the *Boer* and the *Inca*. Both have been broken up long since. When *The Maggie* was filmed, only forty working puffers were left in Scotland, mostly carrying coal, cement or sand. The cost of running on steam, with a crew of four, was becoming crippling. In 1968, the last of the steam-driven cargo puffers was withdrawn from service.

Crinan basin was packed with expensive pleasure boats. Archie, who knows about these things, pointed to a tall metal mast on a yacht. It was a racing mast made of a special alloy.

'That mast alone costs more than your house.'

Next to it was a motor cabin cruiser with the name *Josephine* painted on its glossy white hull. A man in a blazer and yachting cap leaned out, cocktail glass in hand.

'Going far?'

'West over sea,' Archie said poetically, shading his eyes and scanning distant horizons.

'Colonsay,' I said. But what I pictured in my mind was the Corryvreckan.

'Come aboard for a drink.'

We accepted.

Archie said, 'Martin's under age, he'll just have an orange juice.'

We transferred ourselves into the rubber dinghy at the stern and thence onto the *Josephine*. The instrument panel, with its radar screen and two-way radio, was only outdone in splendour by the drinks cabinet and bar. Josephine had been his wife, Bill told us. He had bought the cabin cruiser two years ago to please her, but she had died soon after that. They had never been out in it. In fact, he confessed, he knew nothing about boats or the sea. The prospect of venturing beyond the basin terrified him.

'Why don't you sell it?'

'I couldn't do that. It reminds me of her too much.'

I don't know if he was hoping we'd offer to go with him and show him where 'all those treacherous whirlpools and hidden reefs' were that were waiting to get him. Anyway, we didn't. And, after admiring the engines which he kept in perfect running order, and his works of art on the cabin wall, done from a painting-by-numbers kit, we departed, confirming his worst fears by murmuring things about tide-races, the Dorus Mor, the Corryvreckan and timing being crucial. As we clambered into our canoes, Bill was pouring himself another gin.

Timing was indeed crucial. It was imperative that we arrive at the entrance to the Corryvreckan at the start of, or just before, the slack water which occurs between the end of the westerly tide-race on the flood and the start of the easterly tide-race on the ebb. The timing was doubly crucial because it was a Spring tide. That is to say, it was the time, which occurs twice a month at, or near, new moon and full moon, when the tide rises and falls higher and lower than at other times of the month. (The opposite to a Spring tide is a Neap tide.) It follows that, if a tide has to rise and fall a greater amount within the same time span, it will run faster and, also, the period of slack water will be shorter. Whereas there is one hour of slack water in the Gulf of Corryvreckan at Neaps, there is only a quarter of an hour at Springs. And to paddle through the gulf could well take longer than that!

In one of the earliest accounts of this area are the words, 'Correybreykin is a depe holepoole quhairin if shippis do enter their is no refuge but death on lie.'

Rather less dramatically, the *Clyde Cruising Club Sailing Directions* says: 'This gulf is considered the worst in the West Highlands and strangers are warned against it. The tide sets through at 8 knots Springs and the overfalls caused by the uneven bottom make it extremely dangerous.'

The *Scottish West Coast Pilot* (a different publication from the Admiralty's *West Coast Pilot*) says:

> This passage between Jura and Scarba has a fearsome reputation ... even in calm weather, if the flood is fighting a swell from the west, the Gulf becomes a mass of breaking waves which can overwhelm a small yacht. I do not advise anyone to try the passage, but for those who insist on doing so, arrive about half an hour before the slack which is going to turn against you. This means that, if you are late you are prevented from entering, not sucked helplessly in and through.

Not that Archie and I needed the written word to persuade us to treat it with respect – we had seen it and heard it in full flow. Yet we knew it was possible to go through in a kayak. Others had done it and lived to tell the tale. The weather was calm and, if the timing was right, there should be no real problem . . . so we told each other rather too loudly and too often.

From one point of view the weather was almost too calm. We had regaled Martin with stories of the rough seas and huge swells we would encounter in these parts; we had emphasised how hard it was going to be and how guys like us needed to be really tough to cope with such things; and now here it was, not a breath of air, not a wave insight. Martin was not impressed.

'As smooth as a baby's bum!' he scoffed. 'Well, you should have seen it last time,' we said, unconvincingly.

To reach the Corryvreckan from Crinan we had first to pass through the Dorus Mor, or Great Door, the channel, just north of Crinan, between Craignish Pointon the mainland and the small island of

Garbh Reisa. We had read accounts of the Dorus Mor, of waves
that were 'a jauping popple', of the sea moving through it 'like a
freight train', of bubbling, blistering water and hissing whirlpools.
We, however, were ushered through the door on the comparatively
gentle last two hours of the flood (most tides run for approximately
six hours and build up to their strongest in the third and fourth
hours), experiencing only mild upwelling and fading eddies.

'When does it start getting difficult like you said it would?'
Martin demanded.

At seven in the evening we landed on Jura and rested, preparing for our sprint through the gulf in the quarter hour of slack
water granted to us. The plan was to keep to the south side going
through the gulf and stop for the night at the bothy in Glen
Garrisdale on the west coast of Jura. Then we were off. After
about ten minutes I knew I had made a mistake. We were not
even halfway through the gulf and the current was already
moving against us with considerable force, increasing in strength
at an alarming rate. Quite what the mistake was I could not
understand. Had we landed for our rest in the wrong place? Had
we made a mistake in our calculations? A torrent of water was
now roaring through the gulf. We were barely holding our own,
we would never make it to the other end, that was obvious. But if
we stopped paddling or tried to turn round we might be swept
out of control into the middle of the holocaust.

'Into that bay!' I shouted, and fought my way towards its
narrow entrance.

The sheltered water was no more than fifteen feet away. I
paddled flat out for two, three, four minutes . . . and gained one
foot. Putting my head down, I gave it everything I'd got. My bows
inched forward, but so slowly. Panting, sweating, near to exhaustion, I knew I couldn't keep fighting much longer. Then, my bows
were moving forward faster, and I was into the safety of the bay,
with the others close behind me.

'Now I'm impressed!' Martin announced, as we slumped in
our kayaks, chests heaving.

Next slack water was four in the morning. We were trapped in the bay until then – willing prisoners, for it was a beautiful moon-lit, summer night, the sand was soft, the stars were out – a perfect night for sleeping in the open. We lay there while the heavens slowly revolved, while an otter played in the bay, while the tide unleashed its power, rushing like a mighty river with the eyes of a hundred swirling eddies winking in the moonlight. George Orwell once found himself in difficulties in a rowing boat close to this spot. He was living on Jura, about six miles down the coast at Lealt, while writing *1984*. Which goes to show that there is often no connection between what is going on in an author's head and his/her surroundings. And why had we so nearly got into difficulties? Where had we gone wrong? I wondered.

'Perhaps we should have made an offering to Cailleach, the demoness of the Gulf,' Archie said. At midnight I tuned in to the shipping forecast and discovered that my watch was ten minutes slow. That crucial ten minutes.

Archie recounted the legend of Prince Breckan. To win the hand in marriage of a local princess he anchored his boat in the gulf, intending to stay there for three days and three nights to prove his courage. But the whirlpool swallowed up his boat and he was drowned. A different version has it that his mooring line was made from the plaited strands of his sweetheart's hair, a material which would be unbreakable if she was faithful to him. However, the line parted. The Grey Dog, the strait between Scarba and Lunga, is named after Breckan's dog, who swam ashore from the wreck only to succumb to another ferocious tide-race on the other side of the island.

Four o'clock in the morning, the dawn water flat and gently undulating, tinged pink and orange by the rising sun; fish jumping, their returning plop spreading rings over the glassy surface. Here was our chance to slip from the slackened grasp of the slumbering Corryvreckan without mishap. That was fully our intention as we headed out of the bay.

'Since we're here, what about a wee look at the whirlpool?'

'Before it really gets going, of course.'

'Just a little taste of it.'

The whirlpool develops at the western end of the gulf, near the Scarba shore. Halfway across we could feel the speed pick up. The Scarba shore began moving backwards, faster and faster. A huge blister lifted Martin, then dropped him again; eruptions, depressions, standing waves like solid walls; a growing chaos of water.

The whirlpool! Straight ahead!

It was like a revolving saucer, some twenty feet across, with the outer rim ten feet higher than its centre. I altered course. It filled in and petered out. There it was again, expanding all the time and darting about as it gyrated. However much I altered course, it hunted me. Then it filled in once more and disappeared. I battled with the plunging, bucking, accelerating flow of the gulf, trying, at the same time, to keep a lookout for the whirlpool. Where next? It opened its eye, saw me, reached out and caught me. My bows tilted upwards, the horizon began to spin, I felt myself being dragged backwards into its guzzling vortex. Yesterday I thought I'd paddled as hard as it was possible to paddle. I was mistaken. Then it released me and I was squirted into the ocean beyond the gulf.

Three miles down the west coast of Jura, we ate a second breakfast in Glen Garrisdale. It was only six o'clock. It could have been any time of day as far as I was concerned. In the eye of the whirlpool time had ceased to exist.

'You'll have a few nightmares tonight!' Martin commented.

'I'm afraid I didn't get a photograph,' Archie said. 'Could you do it again?'

A dull roar from the Corryvreckan reached our ears. When a strong westerly wind opposes the outgoing Spring flood through the gulf, the noise can be heard twenty miles down the coast. From our beach we watched that stupendous force of water discharge itself from the narrows and churn like a river for five miles into the ocean.

Dawdling down the coast for a mile or two, admiring the raised beaches, and the three Paps of Jura, we discovered Paradise. The entrance to the bay is a gap of three feet between large boulders; not many craft, other than a kayak or a coracle, are likely to have entered. Behind the bay was a small flower-studded meadow in which a deer grazed, unfrightened by our presence. A waterfall splashed over inland cliffs into a clear pool. Trout darted and flashed in the burn. It is not marked on the map. We named it Paradise Bay. We had a third breakfast consisting of trout tickled from the burn and fried in butter. Once, when camping on the Kintyre Peninsula, a tramp showed me how to do it in return for a cup of tea. You take a stick and scratch around under the boulders until a trout darts out. You watch closely where it next goes into hiding, then very slowly slide your hand, palm upwards, into the water and gently tickle its underside. The effect on the trout is to put it into some kind of paralysed stupor. It rolls over into your hand and lies there quite still while you lift it out.

'What about the code: 'Take nothing but memories'?' Martin asked through a mouthful of wonderfully succulent, delicately flavoured fish.

'Living off the land, at the same level as primitive man, without any modern aids to help you catch your food, doesn't count,' I replied.

'Why not simply admit we enjoy eating trout caught this way, straight from the burn,' Archie said.

§

Next stop Colonsay, a crossing of eighteen miles.

Paddling towards a distant object which is constantly in front of you is a subtle form of torture. You can't forget it's there, you're always conscious of the gap between you and it and of how slowly, how very slowly it is closing. They say that a watched pot never boils. Believe me, a watched island never gets any nearer. After three hours of paddling, the darkish outline that was Colonsay at last revealed some detail: vegetation that looked like bushes, the outline of what might be large boulders. After that, nothing got any bigger. Were it not for the fact that we skimmed past various pieces of flotsam, I would have stopped believing that we were making any progress at all. The sun blazed down on us, punishing us twice over by means of the glare off the smooth surface of the sea. We realised we had not brought nearly enough liquid with us. We became dehydrated and demoralised, stopping more and more frequently for rests that shouldn't have been necessary. In a book written before the war, entitled *Across Hebridean Seas*, Ian Anderson writes: 'Midway between Jura and Colonsay the horizon of the west, north and east becomes rich with a wealth of wonderful seascape and island scenery – a perfect pageant of the Hebrides.' All I can say is that this pageant was wasted on me. I was aware only of my own discomfort and the blasted island that refused to come any closer. In the sixth hour the 'boulders' turned out to be houses and the bushes to be trees.

'Maybe they've grown into trees while we've been crossing,' Martin said. 'They've had long enough!'

Even so, there was still an agonising, cramp-limbed seventh hour to endure. Finally we made land. I eased myself, groaning, out of my kayak, tried to stand upon numb legs and fell backwards into the sea.

Never did water from a burn taste so sweet and cool. After a sleep in the shade we paddled slowly south to Scalasaig where we consumed pints of iced lemonade, ice creams and more lemonade. We had intended to camp on Oronsay which is separated from Colonsay by a tidal ford of golden sand. Oronsay was at one time a sanctuary on which debtors and fugitives from justice were free from arrest. An appropriate place for three unwashed, unshaven ruffians with bank balances in the red. However, at

Scalasaig we heard on the hotel radio that the spell of good weather was breaking. High winds were expected tomorrow. We couldn't chance waiting until then. The prospect of doing the return eighteen miles on the same day did not, in fact, dismay us. Our liquid level and our morale were restored, it was a cool and pleasant evening, and a gentle wind had sprung up to assist us across. The bothy in Glen Garrisdale was our destination. We decided to aim for somewhere along the Jura coast about six miles to the south of it. There were two reasons for this: firstly, it would make the actual crossing shorter; secondly, we would be arriving at Glen Garrisdale in the dark and, therefore, it was better to 'aim off'. If you aim directly at a spot on an unfamiliar coast and fail to hit the target, you are not sure whether to turn left or right. But, if you deliberately aim to one side of it, then, when you arrive at the coastline, you know which way to turn.

There were mice in the bothy. Usually, mice give me the creeps. I've even been known to stand on a chair while my wife escorted a mouse out of our house. That night, however, I slept soundly while they ran all over me. I did dream, though, of the Corryvreckan and its depe holepoole.

Chapter 5

Mad Goats and Welshmen Go Out in the Midnight Moon

Paddling down Loch Lomond

Loch Lomond is Plan B, the bad weather alternative. Storms have been blowing all week and more are promised. The lifeboats along the west coast have been kept busy enough without us adding to their burden. Loch Lomond is the largest inland lake in Great Britain, being some twenty-four miles long and five miles broad at its widest point. Plan B dictates that Martin and I shall do a leisurely paddle down the length of it, starting at Ardlui in the north and finishing at Balloch in the south, with an overnight camp on one of the loch's many islands. Having two cars, one at either end, enables us to make it a one-way trip. Martin has packed a large slab of leek and potato pie which helps us towards a realisation that we are both of Welsh origin. Like the islands in the loch, certain incidents from that weekend stand out. It is only these that I visit here. All the rest is in the space between the words – our steady progress down the loch, the wooded slopes and 'bonny banks', the views of Ben Chabhair, Ben Lomond, Ben Vorlich and Ben Vane; bodies revelling in fresh air and exercise, and minds browsing on anything under the sun; comradeship and laughter. Sudden squalls leaping out at us each time we pass a gap in the hills. A battered armchair stuck in a low branch overhanging the loch; and Martin momentarily believing my explanation that 'it must have been an unusually high tide.' An abandoned cottage on the shore of the loch. Two unshaven men in 'hippy' clothing sitting at a wooden table. One is blindfold, his left hand flat on the table, fingers spread wide. In his right hand a pointed dagger. Thump! Thump! Thump! the knife stabs the table between his fingers. Neither of them returns our greeting. Thump! Thump! Thump! We ascend the bare wooden stairs. Empty rooms, broken windows and a door that won't open. I push harder. It yields as a dead sheep slides out of the way. On a bed lies another dead sheep. Downstairs, the other man is wearing the blindfold, dagger in hand. Thump, thump, thump! We hurry away and take to the water again. Did they, perhaps, think that we were the ghosts?

A speedboat overtakes us, towing a nun on waterskis . . . a nun in full habit, playing the bagpipes. A real nun? Some kind of charity stunt? We never found out.

An island, the size of a magic carpet, grass-covered and perfectly round, its highest point no more than twelve inches above water level. From it I swim the half-mile to the next island, while Martin tows my kayak. Somewhere out in the middle, cold upwellings grip me, take my breath away, rob me of strength, then the water is two or three degrees warmer again.

A shower of rain. A million pearls bouncing on the surface of the water. Droplets sparkling on the kayak deck. A rainbow spanning the loch.

In a channel between two islands we push through a forest of tall, dry, whispering reeds. Wild ducks explode into the air.

Two lovers naked on a lonely shore. We glide past unobserved.

An island campsite in a tree-ringed glade carpeted with pine needles; green-flamed fir-cones sparking in the fire. We decide on a moonlight paddle. As we pass dark islands, birds stir and murmur; the sweet smell of bog-myrtle fills the night air. We slide silently down a silver highway; in front of us a stag swims from one island to another, its antlers silhouetted against the stars.

Back in the tent, we are woken at dawn by a wild goat chewing at the guy ropes and threatening to put its horns through the fabric. I try to discourage it and only succeed in annoying it. It starts butting the tent and knocks it down. I seize it by the horns and wrestle with it. Now it's really mad at me. Although it is probably less than half my weight, its strength is equal to mine. In fact, its strength is greater than mine, I am the one who is tiring first, but I dare not let go of it. Martin manages to slip a rope round its neck and tie it to a tree. We pack the canoes ready to depart, we slide them into the water, we return to the tethered goat, who fixes us with cold yellow eyes. We untie it and run like mad for the kayaks, hotly pursued, becoming waterborne only in the nick of time.

At least the goat has got us up in time to see nature hanging in the balance. A ripening moon sitting exactly on the rim of the eastern hills. A minute later, the moon has sunk from view and the sun has risen.

Fish jumping; a mist lingering on the surface of the water. At times, Martin's kayak is invisible – his body glides above the loch.

The high winds forecast for the whole weekend have not materialised. Perhaps Plan A would have been feasible after all. But we are content with the way things are.

Chapter 6

The Music of the Sea

A trip to Staffa via Iona and Mull

The crossing from Fionnphort to Iona had been short but exhilarating. Some days you know you are on form as soon as you
feel the first wave washing past you. This was one of those days.
The speeding, frolicking green waves, foaming at the crest, were
not a threat but a joy. The colour of the sea had something to
do with it. Forbidding greys make confidence harder to find; but
exactly the same waves in blues and greens, the result of
sunshine or sand below, raise morale and invite adventure. The
Scottish Mountaineering Club Guide says: 'Nowhere are there
greener seas, or whiter sands, or bluer skies than in Iona.' A
statement which is open to argument, perhaps, but Iona does
seem to have this euphoric effect on writers. Ballachulish,
Corran Ferry, the Morven Peninsula, another ferry across the
Sound of Mull, the road to the western tip of the Ross of Mull
– a beautiful drive, but also a long one. But here we were at last,
Archie, Martin and I, poised for our expedition to Staffa. First,
though, we would spend the rest of the day exploring Iona. St
Columba came here from Ireland in AD 563, with twelve
companions, to found a community of religious contemplation
and build a small monastery. Iona was the base from which
Columba introduced Christianity to the Scottish mainland and
islands. The Norsemen ravaged Iona time and again, with the
consequence that the monastery had to be rebuilt several times.
Despite these violent episodes, there is the same atmosphere of

tranquillity about the island that Archie and I had noticed on the Garvellachs.

What I remember best is not the monastery (now referred to as the Abbey), although it is certainly worth a visit, but a scramble high across the face of the sea cliffs. A deep ravine cut into the cliff, halting further progress. It was about ten feet across from rim to rim – not wide enough to back down without feeling humiliated, too wide to jump without hesitation. Actually, that's something of an understatement. We stood on the brink, trying to screw up the courage to do it, listening to the invading sea far below sending up echoing reminders of the distance we would fall. If only the far side was lower instead of higher, if only it didn't slope downwards at such an angle. Supposing . . . There was just room enough to gather speed with half a dozen strides. Each of us had made a run at it . . . and lost his nerve at the last second. Martin started another run . . . he jumped . . . he landed, feet and hands touching ground together, his momentum carrying him forward and away from the edge. Then Archie jumped. My turn. Taking a deep breath, I raced towards the edge, passed the point of no return and launched myself upwards and outwards . . . eternity in one wild heartbeat . . . then I was sprawling on the other side, firmly gripped by two pairs of hands.

That night the tent shivered and shook in a fierce wind. We lay awake, remembering other winds. Once, when climbing Ben More, near Crianlarich, I saw a mountain stream stopped in its tracks by an updraft, vanishing in spray. On the same day, as we crawled on hands and knees from one boulder to another, my companion's rucksack was whipped open, its contents spiralling upwards and over the edge of the pass. About two hours later, we met another climber who described how this book of poetry had fallen out of the sky and landed at his feet. I wish I could say that it fell open at some incredibly significant lines which changed his life. Fraser Darling in his *Island Years,* talking of the fury of the Atlantic gales on North Rona, says: 'I have seen the turf torn from the rocks by the wind and rolled inland, and even stones as big as a man's head pushed from their beds an inch or two deep and rolled two or three yards uphill.' On St Kilda, such was the noise made by storms battering against the island that, according to some accounts, the inhabitants were made deaf for two or three days afterwards. Archie gave us the tale of his attempt to be the first person to cross the desolate Rannoch Moor in a sea kayak. According to the map, it should have been possible, with a few short portages, to link together the dozens of little lochs on the moor into a continuous route. Unfortunately it was one of Scotland's rare periods of drought and the expedition entered the annals of canoeing history in a different way – as the longest distance a sea kayak had ever been carried. I woke later. The wind had died down. I lay listening to the whispering of the water, to its uneasy rise and fall, to its laughter and its singing.

Next morning, with a fine swell running, a legacy of some storm far out in the Atlantic, we set out on the first leg of our triangular route: Iona to Clachandhu on the west coast of Mull, where we would camp for the night, then on to Staffa and back to Iona. Nearing the coast of Mull, the swell steepened as it encountered shallower water, rushing at us sideways on. It is sometimes assumed by the uninitiated that canoes or other small boats which have a deep V shape to their hulls, or a flat, barge like profile, must be more stable than the rounder shape of most sea kayaks. This is not the case. The initial stability for the first few degrees of lean may be greater, but beyond that the more rounded shape of hull, assisted by the hips of the canoeist, is better able to rotate and adjust to the angle of the wave, thus maintaining an upright position. The point being, at this juncture in the story, that the lateral swell was no real threat to us. For the first ten minutes or so our heads were permanently turned left, eyes fixed on the waves. After that we forgot about them, dealing with them instinctively and automatically, our eyes now turned permanently to the right, held there by miles of magnificent cliffs, unfolding headland by headland. There are no roads on this peninsula. Few people see these cliffs from the land, and not many are granted the close-up view from the sea that is possible in a kayak.

Along this coast, just south of the farm at Balmeanach, is MacKinnon's Cave. Nobody has yet found the other end to it. Some say that it penetrates the headland of Burg, coming out at Tiroran. The legend goes that a party set out to find the end of the cave. With them was MacKinnon the piper to play the pipes as the party progressed underground so that another party walking above ground could follow the sound of the pipes and keep track of them. But the explorers encountered a wicked fairy who killed all but the piper. Enchanted by his music she said she would spare his life if he could keep playing till he reached the spot where daylight pierced the gloom of the cavern. The party above the cliffs heard the notes gradually fade away then cease altogether. They clambered down to the mouth of the cave, where they found the dying MacKinnon. Drawing level with the entrance to the cave, we rafted up for a brief rest. A waterfall tumbling over the edge of the cliff curtained the dark interior. The angle of the swell was such that it was running straight into the dark mouth, at times almost filling it. Any ideas we might have had about paddling into the cave were immediately dispelled. From somewhere deep inside the hill there was a persistent booming, like the notes from a giant bass drum. We recalled the time we explored the sea cliffs between Berwick-upon-Tweed and St Abbs Head, north of Eyemouth. On that occasion, each time a swell swept into a cave the increase in air pressure had been painful to the ear.

That evening we scrambled to the top of the cliffs above our campsite. Hebridean islands in a Scottish twilight. Staffa, Little Colonsay, Ulva, Gometra, all the Treshnish Isles. Some views are more than merely a pleasure to the eye, they are deeply felt experiences; they rearrange one's perception of things. The Grand Canyon in Arizona was this kind of experience for me; so were the Himalayas; and the panorama seen from the top of Stob Ghabhar on a clear winter day with visibility extending for at least fifty miles in every direction. The view westwards from Mull was in the same league.

When we set out for Staffa next morning, the swell was still rolling in. We wondered whether we would have any trouble in landing. The day we had gone out to the Bass Rock off North Berwick, the swell had been so big that it had been impossible to get out of our kayaks at the jetty, the only landing-place on the rock. One moment we were six feet below the level of the jetty, the next moment we were way above it. In the end, we swam to the jetty, towing our kayaks. Bob, an acquaintance of ours, who was training for the fifty-mile crossing to St Kilda, told us that he had to be prepared to paddle twice that distance without leaving his kayak because there was the possibility that he might arrive there only to find conditions too dangerous for a landing and have to make the return journey without ever touching terra firma. Twice he set out and turned back halfway out, realising that the weather was deteriorating. I lost touch with Bob and never discovered whether he finally made it all the way or not. In the midst of these speculations, a massive dark shape, about thirty feet long, passed beneath us, some ten feet below the surface. A whale? A giant ray? Whatever it was, it had us swivelling our heads in all directions for the next few minutes, alert and jumpy.

As Staffa drew near, its long, vertical columns of basalt became visible. The Vikings called the island Staffa, which means Stave Island, after their own houses, which were built from tree-logs set vertical. We found a little bay sheltered from the swell and, watched by puffins, succeeded in landing without leaving too many daubs of yellow and orange paint on the boulders. After walking around the island's flat, grassy table-top, we took to the kayaks again and headed for Fingal's Cave.

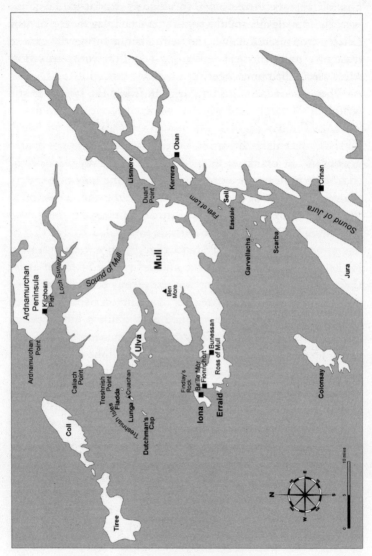

The Ardnamurchan Peninsula,
Mull and surrounding islands

There are steps cut in the stone and railings which make it possible to walk a little way into the cave. A boat-load of tourists was arriving at a small jetty in Clamshell Bay, no doubt with exactly that intention. We paddled faster, wanting the cave to ourselves. At its furthest end, well beyond the cut steps, it was silent, eerie, dripping, booming. The entrance looked like the eye of a black needle. In *Across Hebridean Seas,* Ian Anderson writes:

> There is the deep cave music of the sea, when one feels that the beating of its waves in the depths of a solitary cave echoes the deep notes of the great pipes of a mighty cathedral organ. Many people have never heard this music of which I write, and refuse to believe that the sea can give such music.

We believe you, Mr Anderson.

MacKinnon's Cave – not the same cave as yesterday and not the same MacKinnon either, this MacKinnon being an Abbot of Iona – is bigger than Fingal's Cave, but seldom visited because it is difficult to reach and the entrance is more exposed to rough seas. Except on rare days of absolute calm, only a kayak would be agile enough and seaworthy enough to slip between the surf pounding the guardian rocks. We went in, one by one, each of us trying to time his run through the surf to coincide with a period of smaller waves. Basalt columns arched and soared over us. Fifty yards in – darker, narrower; deep black clefts groaning and sighing, panting like the Minotaur. A giant swell blotted out the entrance. We rose, higher and higher, till it exploded around us, booming and echoing. Then, with waterfalls cascading from every ledge, the swell rushed out again.

On the way back to Iona we passed the tourist boat, whose engine had broken down. Several of the men amongst the passengers had been handed oars. They raised a brave cheer as we overtook them. Somebody on board had a cassette player which sent the strains of Mendelssohn's overture, *Fingal's Cave*, chasing us across the water. But there is nothing quite like the real music of the sea.

Chapter 7

Paddy's Milestone

Visiting Ailsa Craig

'Because it's there' would seem a good enough reason for wanting to make the twelve-mile paddle out to Ailsa Craig. It stands in isolation, rising sheer to a height of 1,114 feet, a fortress sentinel at the entrance to the Firth of Clyde. Lying halfway between Glasgow and Belfast, it was affectionately named 'Paddy's Milestone'. Our point of departure, however, was not Glasgow, but Girvan on the Ayrshire coast. This was an official Scottish Canoe Association meet as advertised in the newsletter. About twenty members were assembled on the beach ready to go. Paddling in large groups with people I don't know is not normally my ideal kind of outing, but I do enjoy the occasional opportunity to meet other canoeists and swap yarns, to observe new techniques, to see the latest equipment in action and generally to exchange information with fellow madmen and masochists. Clusters of canoeists were engaged in animated discussion. It was not of Ailsa Craig they talked, but football. Scotland were playing England that afternoon. The 'Auld Enemie' must be defeated at any cost. The sun was shining. It was going to be a hot day with not much wind to speak of. Most of us stripped down to T-shirts. Two and a half hours was the popular estimate of the time it would take. 'We're off!' came the cry. It was like the start to one of those early motor races, with paddlers running to their craft and climbing into the cockpit. Once out of the shelter of the bay we realised we had been basking in a false sense of security, lulled into thinking it was going to be an easy trip. A force six or seven wind was whipping up the sea, driving it straight at us. Huddles of rafted-up kayaks littered the Firth as people donned their anoraks, some going into all sorts of contortions to extract them from inaccessible places. Then the hard slog began, head on into wind and wave; bows rearing up and crashing down, rearing up and crashing down; waves sluicing up the deck and slapping you in the face; spray flung into your eyes; the cold sea pouring down the front of your anorak, down the back of your neck, up your sleeves; soaked to the skin, something swilling about loose inside the cockpit; hands white, clenched round the paddle, no feeling in your fingers; push, push, push into the wind, force yourself through the opposing waves; longing for a rest but, if you stop, you're swept backwards and lose in two minutes what took twenty minutes of battling to gain.

Bill drew alongside me. 'I should have stayed in the pub and just made up something to tell the guys,' he shouted. 'Not forgetting to add at least ten feet onto the height of the waves . . . the guys automatically subtract that much, anyway.'

At last, five hours later, the party straggled into the little bay near the lighthouse at the foot of Ailsa Craig. Bodies stretched out on the beach, silent and shivering. There was none of the usual banter. A shark cruised around the bay, its fin cutting through the water. Nobody had the energy even to point to it, let alone say anything. The last man in, Bill, staggered white-faced from his kayak.

'What was the score?' he demanded anxiously.

'England won two-nil,' said someone who'd actually listened to his 'tranny' on the way over.

A silence, even more profound than before, settled on the group.

One by one tents sprang up, guy ropes attached to boulders, the ground being too rocky for pegs. Fires were lit from driftwood and old fish boxes. Girvan, Aberdeen, Tarbert, Stranraer were some of the names stamped on their sides. Ivan Boardley of

Ayr and Oban, you have warmed me on this and many another occasion. I thank you for services to canoeists up and down the west coast. Leaving clothes and sleeping bags flapping on lines or festooned over boulders, a group of us set out to explore the island. Beside a steam-driven foghorn was a notice saying 'Noise!' And there was a quarry, the finely speckled granite from which is used in the making of curling stones. From the highest point on the island we could see the Ayrshire coast and all the way down to the Mull of Galloway, and across to the Mull of Kintyre and the coast of northern Ireland. Closer to, we could see the spit on which the lighthouse and our tents were laid out like toys. We watched the hook on the end of the spit gradually change shape as the tide rose. Colonies of gannets and puffins breed on the cliffs of Ailsa Craig. We looked down on thousands of gliding, soaring wings catching the evening sun, matching the white horses on the waves even further below. Then, from hundreds of feet up, a pair of wings would fold as a gannet plummeted into the sea. Fishermen have reported finding gannets entangled in their nets as much as 100 feet beneath the surface. The puffins were out in force too. Known variously as 'bottle nose', 'Tommy noddy', or 'sea parrot', the puffin has declined in numbers on Ailsa Craig because of oil slicks and because rats have come ashore from a recent wreck. We didn't have time, before the light faded, to explore the Water Cave by Stranny Point which leads into the heart of the rocky isle; nor Goat Cave that used to shelter the goats that supplied milk to the lighthouse-keepers.

That night, a group of bird-watchers, who had come over in a hired boat, joined the singing round the bonfire. With the malt whisky that had been doing the rounds still glowing inside me, but the embers of the fire fast fading, I chose to abandon my tent and sleep deep in the bracken amongst the fragrance of purple campion, bluebells and white arctic vetch. Pebbles chattered on the beach, the lighthouse's beam flashed in and out of my dreams.

Next morning, it started to rain as I was eating my breakfast. I stood there in my anorak, hood up, while the drizzle diluted the canned milk in my cereal. After a circumnavigation of the island, we were wafted homewards by a following swell, travelling at twice the speed of yesterday. Soon the rain stopped and dazzling white clouds dropped their shadows on the Ayrshire hills; the coast was a patchwork of sunlit greens into which sails cut white notches. About halfway across, a nuclear submarine appeared as a black dot in the distance, heading for the open sea. In no time at all it was a bulbous black monster, tearing past us, throwing up an immense wash with all the nasty characteristics of a tidal wave. This vast wall of water roared towards us, breaking at the top. My bows lifted almost vertically. For a moment I thought I was going to loop over backwards. Indeed, two kayaks in the group did exactly that. One managed an Eskimo-roll and brought himself upright again. The other we rescued by forming a raft with our kayaks on either side of his upturned craft.

In the car park near the beach, the group began to disperse. Here and there addresses were exchanged. A lump of barren rock sticking out of the sea had brought us together and united us. An island is a good place to learn that no man is an island.

Chapter 8

Iron and Gold

A wreck in the Clyde Estuary

Iron Island

On the morning of Monday 28th January 1974, a new landmark appeared in the Clyde Estuary. A 4,500 ton Greek cargo ship lay on her side between Helensburgh and Greenock. An island called *Captayannis*. During the night, in a 60 m.p.h. gale, the *Captayannis* had dragged her mooring and drifted in heavy seas before colliding with a tanker and being holed. In a bid to save his ship, the Greek captain deliberately ran her onto a sandbank. Later that morning, as 8,000 tons of sugar dissolved in the Clyde, the captain bowed to the inevitable and abandoned her. Slowly the deserted ship settled onto her side, coming to rest at a perfect ninety degrees to her upright position. The *Captayannis* lies there to this day, in mid estuary. The iron cliffs of her underside are turned towards the Greenock shore, her decks face Helensburgh. The bows point upriver, while beyond the stern is the Gareloch and the wild hills of Argyll. Every year the reds and browns of rust are more apparent; every year she is a little greener about the water-line, whiter from bird-droppings. Meanwhile the legal wranglings continue about who should be responsible for moving the hulk. Known locally as the Sugar Ship, the wreck of the *Captayannis* is now a familiar and well-liked feature of the Clyde. On a spring day, I decided to take a closer look at her. I launched my kayak from the Helensburgh shore and paddled towards the low, sombre shape. I drew nearer. Her mast lay exactly along the surface of the water; ship and tide in perfect equilibrium. Decks were walls, walls were decks, while ladders walked horizontally into space. Momentarily I felt I was a bird hovering above the ship. So strong was the illusion of verticality that I began toppling sideways in my canoe.

The well-deck towered above me. A hatch opened like a window into the cavernous hull. I peered inside. Black, black water, the stench of oil and rust and a hollow, dripping sound. That hold had contained a full cargo of sugar. Had the sea tasted sweet, I wondered, and what had the fishes made of it?

I passed under a cable dangling from a block. Overhead, the lifeboat davits swung empty. The lifeboats had not been used but salvaged after the ship had gone aground.

Turning towards the stern I paddled into the gloomy canyon between the upper and lower decks. My craft bumped a submerged girder; my blade snared in a mass of rusty chains. Entangling shapes lurked beneath me. It was too narrow to turn. Cautiously I backed out again.

Slowly I cruised the length of the wreck. The funnel was a vast gullet. A wave ran up it and gurgled into darkness. The starboard bow, rearing high, but gently sloping at the water-line like a little beach. Then, round to what had been the ship's underside. She was flat-bottomed with iron cliffs of rusty brown. Clouds of seabirds rose at my approach. Passing between the stern and the green conical buoy marked 'Wreck', I completed a circuit of the *Captayannis*.

Boarding her was difficult. With the help of a spar and a half-submerged companionway, I eased out of my kayak. A rucksack containing food, clothes and a sleeping bag followed me aboard. I was going to spend a night on the wreck. Edging along the handrail of a ladder I gained a foothold on a porthole and pulled myself onto the side wall of the upper bridge. From there I walked onto the grey hull, amazed at how flat it was.

I wandered over the steel-riveted plateau, admiring the view. South-eastwards, over the bows, was the wooded Ardmore Point;

from the stern, a panorama of sea lochs and the sun setting behind the mountains of Argyll.

Ringed by the twinkling lights I ate my meal. Then, moving back to the bridge I climbed through an opening and dropped into the wheelhouse. In the centre of the floor was a porthole; in the middle of one wall a door opened like a letter-box. The wheel itself, the compass and other instruments of navigation were gone. After the abating of the storm on that wild night, swarms of little boats had clustered round the dead ship. In a matter of days, furniture, fittings – anything movable – had disappeared.

I unrolled my sleeping bag in a corner and prepared for sleep. It was dark. It was cold. The ship let out a long, deep sigh. I listened intently. She rumbled and echoed and made strange sighing sounds. The changing tide, I told myself. Volumes of air and water shifting inside her, I told myself. I did not believe it. I lay thinking of that January storm. It must have been at about this hour that the *Captayannis* had broken from her moorings and collided with the giant tanker. With water gushing into her port ballast tanks and a list developing, it would have been from the radio room below me – no, beside me – that they had called for help. It was probably from this very room that the captain and his four officers had finally been rescued on that fateful night. Dawn was breaking. The sea was flat calm; and the gulls were resting in their hundreds on the hull.

Since that first visit I have returned to the *Captayannis* many times. I have picnicked on her; I have sought shelter in her lee; and I have watched the moss take root in her primitive soil of bird-droppings, windblown dust and peeling paint. Last year I saw the first sea pinks bloom. The arguments about salvaging her continue. I hope they continue for a long time yet. I've grown fond of *Captayannis,* our iron island in the Clyde.

Golden Isle

Tides swept me to an isle emerging from the sea;
I laughed and splashed through pools which shone
And end to end made footprints in the sand –
My golden isle, revealed to me alone.
But I forgot that all tides turn,
That loss will follow find.
On dwindling ground I stayed too long,
My tracks dissolving one by one
Till at the end, I nearly drowned.
Those sands now lie so deep, so many fathoms down.
Can it be? Can it really be?
Will time erase that imprint in the depths of me?

Chapter 9

Never on a Sunday

Instructor assessment off the coast of Lewis

I did not know it then, but the trip to Staffa was the last time Archie, Martin and I were ever to canoe together. Martin was sent on business to Abu Dhabi and Archie's life was changed by a terrible tragedy. His son was paralysed from the neck downwards as the result of a motorbike accident, and helping to look after him left no time for canoeing. Unexpectedly, I found myself without any regular canoeing partners. So, when I received an invitation from Stornoway Canoe Club on Lewis to come as a guest instructor and tester, I gladly accepted. The ten-day meet was to be based in a disused schoolhouse near Valtos, Loch Roag, on the west coast of Lewis. When I say that I accepted the invitation gladly, that doesn't mean it was not without some trepidation. The west coast of Lewis is unprotected by offshore islands and exposed to the full Atlantic swell. Winds from the west have a fetch of 2,000 miles or more in which to generate horrendous seas. There are almost no pleasure boats this side of Lewis and the islanders themselves seldom venture onto the sea in these parts, regarding it as dangerous and malevolent. Loch Roag is like an oasis between two stern environments, the sea and the notorious Black Moor of the interior with its bare rock, barren heath and innumerable dark lochans. From the top of the cliffs of Gallan Head, on a sunny day, Loch Roag appears as a great irregular sheet of blue water, bejewelled by little emerald isles. W. H. Murray in his book *The Hebrides* describes its 'lark-loud machair bright with flowers' and how 'prongs of gneiss run out through a brilliant green sea, deepening to dark mauve.' From the same cliffs the Flannan Isles can be seen, twenty-one miles to the north-west. Sometimes called 'The North Hunters' or 'The Seven Hunters', they are the site of the first lighthouse this side of the Atlantic. Many years ago an unsolved mystery occurred when all three keepers disappeared without trace from the lighthouse, leaving a partially eaten meal on the table.

My main task was to run a course for the five most experienced members of the club, Alan, Ian, Ian, Ian and Dave, who wanted to take the Advanced Sea Kayaking Certificate, and to assess them at the end of the course. All of them had learned their canoeing in the rough seas around Lewis. Almost from the moment they'd sat in a kayak they had been coping with advanced conditions. But I needed to see for myself what they could do, how they would deal with emergencies and with stress, if they knew how to work as a team and how to help each other. Most important of all was the ability to plan and lead a long trip. The key question I asked myself about each one of them was, would I be completely confident about going on a trip led by this person; would I put my life in his hands?

There was no need to go looking for suitably testing conditions, they were never less than testing – right from the first minutes when each day started with a battle through the surf that thundered into the bay. And there was any number of headlands along the coast only too ready to oblige with mountainous seas moving all ways at once in a chaos of colliding waves and sudden chasms. Gallan Head, the most exposed buttress on this coast, was particularly 'interesting'. Brian Wilson, who made a remarkable solo journey round Scotland by kayak, likens the rounding of Cape Wrath to being 'a flea on the rump of a great bull elephant in the midst of a herd orgy'. I don't suppose Gallan Head was even half as fierce as Cape Wrath, but I know what he means. And, after Gallan Head, the following passage from Neil

Gunn's *The Silver Darlings* immediately struck a chord inside me when I read it:

> He had heard of a Gaelic poem that described all the different kinds of waves there are. But no poem could describe them all. Take this one coming at them now – now! – its water on the crest hissed into little waters, running, herding together, before – up, up! Over its shoulder and down into the long flecked hollow like a living skin. Or that one steaming off there! – A great lump of ocean, a long-barbed ridge overtopping all, a piled up mountain!

I would guarantee that the author wrote that from first-hand experience. In the midst of all this, an exhausted bumble bee flopped onto my deck. What it thought it was doing out there, I don't know. Although, I must say, I was beginning to wonder what I was doing out there myself. Anyway, I was too preoccupied with my own survival and with keeping an eye on all the others to pay it much attention. The next time I could spare a glance, it was gone.

A strong incentive for subjecting ourselves several times to the ordeal of Gallan Head was the beautiful bay of Camas Uig which lay to the west of it. Its mile-long sweep of brilliant white sands is a mosaic of tiny shells of extreme fragility and delicacy of colour, pinks and purples, lilac, orange, yellow, lemon. In 1831 a crofter walking home along these sands discovered, buried in a dune, a collection of walrus ivory chess pieces of Viking origin. I play chess regularly with a friend who has a set of these squat twelfth-century Norsemen, not carved from ivory but moulded from a modern resin ... much the same material, in fact, as impregnates and bonds the fibreglass of my kayak, whose design is of Eskimo origin, older even than the Viking long ship that must have brought the chessmen to Lewis.

All along the west coast of Lewis are headlands, buttresses, arches and stacks. Robert Louis Stevenson, writing of these stacks, the result of collapsed caves and arches, said: 'There they stand, for all the world like their neighbours ashore; only salt water sobbing between them instead of the quiet earth, and clots of sea pink blooming on their sides instead of heather, and the great sea-conger to wreathe about the base of them instead of the poisonous viper of the land.' These coastal features were a constant lure to us. Seen from the land, Lewis may be dark and grim and treeless, a land scraped bare by glaciers, but from the sea, its variety of cliff scenery and rock formations is fascinating, all the more so because, as the tide shifts, no one place is ever quite the same. I recall one outing to some sea caves. On the way there, steep, dark walls dropped sheer into an ink-black sea which grumbled and sulked and sighed heavily around the lower ramparts. The return journey at low tide was quite different. A fresh new coastline had been created, glistening with green, brown and red algae and populated by sea anemones and starfish. The rock was no longer dark, but studded with white molluscs. Islands and reefs had appeared, around which the sea swashed and seethed and behaved in an entirely different manner from before. The same caves into which we had canoed earlier now hung open-mouthed above the water-line.

Of the caves themselves I recall shags hurtling out of the darkness, passing low overhead; nests high up on ledges; the slap of the waves against the confining walls and the cries of the birds combining in an eerie echo; a window onto the sky in the roof of a cave; canoeing in one way and out through another; narrow passages and archways best traversed on the forward surge of a wave; cormorants diving near a cave mouth, entering the water at eighty miles an hour, pursuing their prey underwater, twisting and turning.

On another day, we did a trip in the comparatively sheltered waters of Loch Roag, threading a route between the islands to Callanish. One small uninhabited island was featureless except for a red postbox.

'Maybe the Loch Roag seals have learnt to read and write,' suggested one of the Ians.

'Consult tide tables for the annual collection date.'

'Post early for the next Christmas but one!'

I wish, now, that I had sent myself a letter from there.

Rounding an island, we surprised two fishermen mending salmon nets. They were so clearly discomforted by this chance meeting that we surmised they must be poachers. After fighting the strong current which surged under the bridge between Great Bernera and Lewis (a black mark to the person whose turn it was to lead the group and do the calculations), we landed on the shores of East Loch Roag and walked over boggy ground to the ancient standing stones of Callanish. These megaliths date from about 1500 BC – two centuries before the Egyptian pyramids – and are thought to be the remains of a Bronze Age sun temple. Herodotus refers to it as 'the Great Winged Temple of the Northern Isles'. What the bus-load of Japanese tourists made of the strangely dressed group which appeared out of nowhere from a roadless tract of land, I don't know. On the way back to our kayaks we passed a man cutting peat. I lingered to watch him. He addressed me in Gaelic and was annoyed when I didn't understand him.

'The most ancient language in Europe and you haven't both-ered to learn a single word!' he said in English. 'If you had been on holiday in France or Spain you'd be saying a phrase or two, wouldn't you?' I mumbled an apology and asked him about the peat.

'Ah, the wonder of peat is that it warms you five times over! . . . When you cut it, when you turn it for the drying, when you load it, when you stack it and finally when you burn it.'

I told him that we were canoeists and made some remark about the strength of the wind in these parts. These were mere breezes, he informed me, compared to what happened in winter. Then, the roar of the sea and the spray hitting his window kept

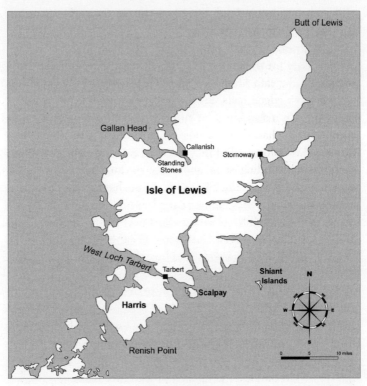

The Isle of Lewis

him awake at night, even though his cottage was three-quarters
of a mile inland. And ten-foot drifts blocked the road.

'Snow drifts?'

'No, sand, blown by the wind.'

I told him that we would probably attempt the Butt of Lewis
the next day if the weather was right.

He gave me a long, hard stare. 'You'll not be doing anything
tomorrow . . . It's the Sabbath, have ye forgotten that?'

When I joined the others on the beach, they agreed that canoeing on a Sunday was out of the question.

'Hill walking would be all right, though,' Alan said. 'The local villagers wouldn't mind that. Out on the water you're too visible. It's being seen that matters.'

Sunday. We drove to the Butt of Lewis 'just for a wee peek at it from the cliffs'. Beneath walls of black gneiss, ocean rollers seethed amongst saw-edged reefs. Further out, a strong tidal stream from the Atlantic ran slap into one hurrying north from the Minch and another which had been travelling northwards up the east side of Lewis. The resulting collision at the crossroads was an intimidating sight. In this brooding island abounding in cairns, duns, brochs and standing stones, it is difficult not to believe that the old Celtic gods live on. In ancient times, human sacrifice had been made to the sea-god Shoni. People had been thrown to him from this very spot. Maybe, these days, he relied on foolhardy canoeists for his dues.

'Just our luck it's a Sunday!' exclaimed an Ian. And we nodded and frowned and avoided each other's eyes.

That evening, inside the schoolhouse, Alan produced his guitar. He sang the Canadian Boat Song, composed by some anonymous exile from the Outer Hebrides who had been forcibly shipped out to Canada to make way for sheep:

> From the lone shieling of the misty island
> Mountains divide us, and the waste of seas;
> Yet still the blood is warm, the heart is Highland,
> And we in dreams behold the Hebrides.

Amongst the other songs Alan sang was a poem (author unknown to me, I'm afraid) which he'd set to his own music:

> No rest from restless will
> And hot desire;
> We take the tide at the fill
> Tho' the gale's higher,
> Knowing, when winds grow still,
> So does the fire.

Monday. The wind most definitely had not grown still. No Butt of Lewis today. As we headed out of our bay on a training exercise, I began putting my advanced group through its paces. Each of the five in turn would be given a problem to deal with. It would be up to him to organise the others. Suddenly I capsized and, after a while, floated to the surface, face down, apparently unconscious. While the others rafted up beside Dave to give him stability, he hauled me across his cockpit and went through the motions of giving the kiss of life. In days gone by, the fishermen in these parts used to perform a similar ritual, a kind of imitative magic, in which one of their number would be thrown out of the boat and then hauled in again as if he were a fish. Another quarter of a mile on I developed symptoms of hypothermia. Alan, in my opinion, acted correctly in ensuring that I used up no more heat and energy in paddling. After I had been wrapped in extra clothing and put into a survival bag, someone was appointed to sit alongside me in his kayak and hold me upright while the others shared the towing. Alan did not offer me anything from his flask of hot tea. Current thinking on hypothermia is that alcohol or hot drinks dilate the blood vessels and take heat away from the body's central core, which is the bit that matters most. One wonders how many people were finished off rather than saved by those St Bernard dogs with kegs of brandy round their necks. Having recovered from hypothermia, I then suffered severe leg cramps; and then my kayak struck a floating timber and was badly holed. The simulated problems and the discussion of how they were handled continued throughout the day. Mostly it was I who played the part of victim because I wanted all the others involved in finding solutions. Approaching Valtos Bay, but still more than a mile and a half out, we heard the thunder of a gigantic surf. One mile away and it became visible, white with rage. Half a mile in, we began to feel the urgency of the waves in their quest to smash themselves upon the beach. They careered to their destruction with ever-increasing speed, curling at the top, rushing towards the moment when their tottering structure would collapse. Every second, the angry roaring grew louder, nearer. I was seized and hurled forward like a dart. A long sea kayak is not built for surf. The back and top of a surf wave is continually trying to overtake its front and if your kayak is long enough to be in both parts of the wave at once, horrible things happen. I was suddenly whipped sideways to the steep, foaming wall. Thrusting my paddle deep into its heart, I leant on the wave with the main bulk of it under my armpit like a cushion. Now, totally in the power of the surf, I hurtled sideways for about 200 yards before being catapulted forward so precipitously that my kayak somersaulted, crashing me head downwards onto the sand. Half-stunned, winded, shaken, I tried to get out of the kayak, but a fierce undertow dragged me out to sea once more. Again I was hurled towards the beach, again I was dumped head first with my kayak on top of me. As the undertow claimed me for a second time, I lost interest in what was happening to me.

Why was I doing a head-stand with my feet against a wall? Only I wasn't – I was lying on my back on the sand, with a circle of faces round me. Alan told me what had happened. They had all thought that this was another of my pretend situations. They had lounged on the beach admiring my performance.

'He's really excelling himself this time!' Dave had said. Luckily for me, alarm bells had begun to ring in their brains and they dashed into the 'soup' and pulled me out.

'Just because you saved my life, don't think you're all automatically going to pass the test!' I growled, a trifle embarrassed that the only one not to come through the surf successfully was me, the instructor.

'Shall we give him back to the sea now or later?' Alan asked.

Tuesday. I was feeling a bit too delicate to lead an attempt on the Butt of Lewis. Wednesday, Thursday and Friday – the weather was too unsettled to try it. Saturday, the last day of the course, was taken up with the official test, the personal interviews, the written paper on navigation, etc . . . They all passed, by the way.

'We could stay on an extra day to have a go at the Butt,' a couple of Ians suggested.

'Not on a Sunday. Never on a Sunday!' chorused the others.

I agreed. Not entirely out of respect for the islanders or the Maker who rested on the seventh day. Out there was another god, Shoni, who had been cheated of his sacrificial victim.

Chapter 10

Journey to the Moon

Across the Minch to the Monach Isles

A solo crossing of the Minch has to be approached with caution. The *Clyde Cruising Club Sailing Directions* states: 'It is advisable to pick the weather for crossing the Minch at any part, as in bad weather the seas can be *very* bad.' Thus it was that I camped for three days at Trumpan on the Vaternish Peninsula of Skye, waiting for a settled spell of weather. As the saying has it, the decision about going was 'weather or no'. Geoffrey Winthrop Young, one of the greatest pioneers of British mountaineering, in his classic book *Mountain Craft,* calls the weather 'the background, foreground, and middle distance of all big mountaineering'. The same is true for sea kayaking. Winthrop Young had to rely on observing the signs and applying traditional wisdom such as:

> Mackerel skies and mares' tails
> Make great ships carry small sails.

Or:

> When the swallow flies low
> Fine weather must go.

I can't say I ever found this kind of weather lore very helpful. The only one that ever seems to work for me is the one that says something like 'if you can't see your local landmark it means it's raining, and if you can see it, you're lucky because it soon will be.'

But the following jingle definitely does work:

> When satellites are flying the sky
> There's tales of pressures low and high.
> So carry small change and don't risk all
> Unless you've made that vital phone call.

As a jingle it doesn't work very well, but as good advice it does. At the time of my trip to the Monach Isles the instant weather reports by telephone from services such as Marine Line, Mountain Line, or Weatherline were not available, but a phone call to a coastguard station or to the Glasgow Airport weather station provided the required information. Of course, there were also the regular shipping forecasts on the radio, but I seemed to have the knack of missing them.

I had considered making the crossing via the Shiant Isles, whose name in Gaelic means Enchanted Isles, a place of soaring basalt columns and a breeding ground for puffins. However, all around the Shiants, because of the shallower waters and the irregular bottom, there are heavy overfalls. My blue-bound 'bible' on these matters informed me: 'In bad weather or when a heavy swell is running, this part of the Minch should be avoided altogether, as it is considered the most dangerous part between the Butt of Lewis and Barra.' Not a place, I thought, for a person alone in a kayak. So, I decided on the shortest and most direct route across, from Dunvegan Head on Skye to Loch Maddy on North Uist, a distance of approximately fourteen miles.

One particular cautionary tale had stuck in my mind concerning the Minch: a sea kayaker of my acquaintance, Sam, was canoeing along the north coast of Skye with a friend when the latter said (jokingly, as it turned out), 'Let's cross the Minch.' Sam did not want to be the one to chicken out, so he called his friend's bluff. And changing course, off they set. Each kept

A fish farm on the west coast.
(All photographs from the Author's Collection unless otherwise stated)

Waterlilies on Loch Lomond.

Fingal's Cave, Staffa.

Rum seen from Eigg.

Captayannis, the wrecked sugar ship in the Clyde estuary.

Captayannis has been left to rust slowly.

Landing on the Treshnish Isles.

On the Treshnish Isles. Left to right: Colin, Robin, Ian and Archie.

Loch Fyne. Tea break on a raw, wet day.

Cockle banks at Cardross.

Craigendoran sands on a summer evening.

No camp is complete without a driftwood fire.

Corryvreckan whirlpool, between Jura and Scarba.

Rounding Raasay. Skye in the background.

Orkney. Shall we do it or not?

Seals on North Ronaldsay.

Entering a Shetland cave. (Ian Smith Collection)

This Shetland cave exits further down the coast. Beware of a swell!

Approaching Mukkle Flugga, Shetland. (Ian Smith Collection)

A million miracles a minute.

Jellyfish on the beach.

So many delights along the shore.

Time for reflection on Loch Etive.

Sunset on Loch Sunart.

expecting the other to declare that he hadn't really meant it and to call off the crossing. But they were both too proud and stubborn, and so they paddled on and on into roughening seas. The crossing took eleven hours. At last, somewhere on a beach in Harris they lay in near-darkness, totally exhausted, lucky to be alive. Only then did they confess to each other that neither had really wanted to do it. Sam had been wearing a wet-suit and suffered big raw patches under his armpits where the tight-fitting suit had chafed him. But, as he said, 'It was a small price to pay for such stupidity'.

I was certainly hoping for rather less than an eleven hour crossing – depending on the wind, something around five hours, perhaps. When I had been on Lewis, instructing with the Stornoway Canoe Club, I had met John and his wife Mallig. They had come up from South Uist to join the course. Although John did not take the Advanced Certificate during these ten days, he was an experienced paddler and, more importantly, a compatible soul, a person with whom I could paddle for hours on end and always find something interesting to talk about. John and I had arranged to meet at Loch Maddy (I would phone just before setting off) and from there we were aiming for the Monach Isles, a small group of islands eight miles west of North Uist. Excitement flowed through me at the thought of paddling to somewhere even further west than the main bulk of the western isles. It seemed like the edge of the known world. Near my tent on the Vaternish Peninsula a man and his wife had parked their car and were sitting inside it admiring the scenery. I could see them discussing me and my kayak. The man stepped out of the car and, shivering in the wind like a tortoise removed from its shell, came over to me. He and his wife visited Skye every year, he told me, 'to get away from the rat race on the mainland'.

'We often just sit in the car and look at the sea. We love the sea.'

He enquired about my destination.

'The Monach Isles,' I said.

He hadn't heard of them. I showed him on the map.

'It might as well be the moon as far as I'm concerned,' he said wistfully. 'I know I'll never get to a place like that.'

His wife called him back. I heard her saying, 'I hope he knows what he's doing.'

Finally, the shipping forecast on the radio and the local coastguard both agreed that conditions were right for a reasonably safe crossing. The latter, of course, had been well advised of my plans and I had a number to phone on arrival at the other side. And so, on a clear morning, with the Minch breathing gently in its sleep, I passed the black cliffs of Dunvegan Head and set course for Loch Maddy. North Uist was no more than a thin pencil-line south of the purple hills of Harris. Behind me was the jagged blue-black barrier that forms the skyline – the Cuillin Hills. To my right, and out in the middle of the Minch, were the Shiants, from this angle like two lazy dogs basking in the sun. A century ago, the crofters from Loch Shell on Harris made expeditions to the Shiants for puffins. Boiled puffin was considered a welcome change to the usual diet of fish and oats, also the feathers were valued for insulation.

The men would lie on their backs on the steep slopes of the islands and simply whack the puffins with their fishing rods as they flew past, quite low and in their tens of thousands. Whether the puffins were killed or only stunned they would roll down the slope onto the beach where the rest of the crew gathered them into the boat. The Minch, in different conditions, is a tremendous challenge to canoeists, but on this occasion there are no adventures to tell. While the Minch flirted with a sweet and gentle breeze, I slipped across in four hours, passing between two rocks, Madach Beag and Madach Mor, the two Maddies, which guard the entrance to Loch Maddy.

John met me on the pier at Loch Maddy. His own kayak was pulled up on the beach not far away. I made my phone call to the coastguard. Then, to stretch my legs, we walked a couple of miles down the road and up a small hill called Blashaval. From this vantage point Loch Maddy resembles an octopus. It has so many arms and inlets that its shoreline totals 400 miles. The whole of this north-east coast is a maze of peninsulas and little islets so that there is almost more land than water; and then, looking south from the hill, the scene is reversed. The island of North Uist appears to be more water than land, a network of a hundred fresh-water lochs and lochans. North Uist, isle of lochs and sea of isles.

Returning from our walk, we got into conversation with a fisherman at the pier whose father remembered the days when a whaling station had operated on the shores of West Loch Tarbert on Harris. Up to the beginning of World War I it was in full operation, the whaling grounds for this station extending from St Kilda to beyond the Butt of Lewis.

Our planned take-off point for the Monach Isles was Hougharry on the north-west coast of North Uist. I had proposed that we camp the night there, then start out next morning. The distance round the north end of North Uist via the Sound of Berneray to Hougharry was nearly forty miles.

'Well, we'd better get started,' said John, picking up his kayak and walking towards the water. Then he stopped and laughed.

'As a matter of fact, the car is just round the corner. You're spending the night in our house and then we'll drive to Hougharry tomorrow . . . I'm really looking forward to the trip, it'll be such a relief to get away from the rat race on the Uists.'

Butterflies stirred in my stomach and gave a flutter or two as we set off into the wide expanses of the ocean, our destination below the horizon, nothing ahead but Atlantic and more Atlantic and rolling slate-blue downs being ploughed and reshaped by a westerly force five wind. I had discovered already, from the Lewis days, that force five was a sort of base line. On the exposed side of the Outer Isles it seldom fell below that; the only question was, how much stronger than five would it be? Waves washed over my bows each time my kayak buried its nose in a lump of water. We thumped our decks in time to the sea, in time to our song, and bawled into the wind:

> With days at their worst to hinder and harry me,
> Summerland calls, and naething shall tarry me;
> Wind from the dawning sun westward shall carry me
> Back to the Islands of Glory.

> There's glory of sun and glory of thundering,
> Glory of storm that I worship in wondering;
> Glamour of cities will no more be sundering
> Me from the Islands of Glory.

After an hour of paddling, a black needle pricked the skyline. This was the lighthouse on Shillay, the most westerly of the Monach Isles. There are five main islands in the group. From west to east they are: Shillay, Ceann Iar (West Head), Shivinish, which is joined to it by a tongue of sand at low tide, Ceann Ear (East Head), which is the largest, being about two and three quarter by one and three quarter miles in dimension, and Stockay. The legend in these parts is that the Lost Continent once linked the Monach Isles, St Kilda and the Seven Hunters (Flannan Isles). In 1891 the population reached its highest recorded level of 135 persons. Their livelihood was supplemented by the sharp teeth surrounding the islands which snapped up the occasional wreck and brought bounty to their shores, and by the Gulf Stream which carried to them wreckage from far and wide. However, the population slowly declined after that; in 1942 the lighthouse on Shillay was abandoned and in 1943 the islands became uninhabited when the last remaining family took fright after a particularly severe storm and left.

The needle grew taller, but still no land was visible. Neither John nor I knew quite what to expect. That it would be exposed and hostile we took for granted. The Gaelic names on the old maps and charts said as much: Ru' na Marbh (Death Point), Sgeir

Mhor (Big Rock), Sillay (Rainy Island), na Diurabegs (small difficult rocks). Each time we rose on a wave, a dark horizontal line was now discernible, which slowly focused and became separate islands, until, near the end of the third hour of paddling, we could identify Ceann Ear, the biggest island, and steer towards it. And then messages reached us on the wind which belied all those hostile names, clover-scented messages, the flower-sweet breath of the Monach Isles.

Standing on a sand dune tufted with marram grass, I looked back at the 'Long Isle' of Lewis, Harris, North Uist, Benbecula, South Uist and Barra, forming one continuous misty line. 'It might as well be the moon,' the man had said, and he was right, for it was, indeed, like looking at the earth from another planet. An Argonaut, a Robinson Crusoe, a moon walker – I was all these things; and I was a newborn babe, seeing flowers and colours for the very first time. 'Except a man be born again he cannot enter the Kingdom of God.' For surely this was part of that kingdom. Machair and meadowland, the island was a magical carpet of flowers unrolled on an empty sea. Red fescue, sandwort, speedwell, birds foot trefoil, ragwort, wild thyme, bedstraw, lady's smock, harebell, heart's-ease, eye bright, red clover, white clover, yellow buttercups, blue buttercups and daisies galore. Butterflies, not the same ones that had been in my stomach, flitted across the machair.

> Until a man has seen a good machair, like that of Berneray, of the Monach Isles, or of Tiree, he may find it hard to realise that although the crofters call it 'gress' it grows not grass but flowers . . . In May the main body of the machair puts out its flowers in annual order, daisies first, buttercups soon after, then blue speedwell and yellow birds foot trefoil, the others following till the green turf is almost lost to sight under blossom . . . I have been to Toe Head isthmus in Harris when it was wholly under daisies; it blazed like a snowfield, and half an hour later flushed pink as the cups closed in response to cloud and a sharpening wind.

So writes W. H. Murray, and I most certainly agree with him that the machair of the Monach Isles is one of the finest in the Western Isles.

We explored the ruined houses on Ceann Ear. The old schoolhouse is still used by Uist fishermen who come out here in the summer for lobsters and flounders. We took a quick look inside. There were two bunks, one surrounded by pictures of half-dressed women in erotic poses, the other by reproductions of Braque and Picasso; on a table between the two, girlie magazines and religious tracts mingled. There were lockers full of food and a field telephone powered by solar batteries. Outside the schoolhouse was the huge, bleached vertebra of a whale, large enough to use as a table. Later, the fishermen anchored their diesel-driven boat in the same bay in which we were camping. At first they were reserved, regarding us as interlopers. Clearly, they did not believe we had canoed across. They thought we must have been brought by a bigger boat and were just using the kayaks to potter around the islands. When we convinced them that we had indeed made the crossing, their whole attitude changed, there was respect in their voices as they plied us with the pick of their catch. The fresh lobsters made excellent eating, but even more pleasing to me was that our seamanship had been recognised by hardened professionals. The fishermen had thrown out several conger-eels which had got into the creels. Some they cut up for bait, the others they left on the sand.

'I never eat them,' said the Picasso-lover, 'too much of the snake about them!'

As an appetiser before the lobsters, I tried a slice, fried in butter.

'What's it like?' John asked.

'Like rubber washers fried in butter.'

I left a chunk of eel boiling for two hours before again frying it in butter.

'What's it like now?'

'Like rubber washers which have been boiled for two hours, then fried in butter.'

That night, lying in the tent, we heard seals singing, not unlike a dog keening, not unlike the wind, but more musical, more evocative. In former days, many folk in the Outer Hebrides believed seals to be human beings under enchantment. We remembered too that Heisker, to give the islands their Norse name, were the abode of the supernatural water horse and a special place for 'the little people'.

Dodging between the islands the next morning was a series of brief but exciting tussles with rip tides and disturbed waters which were being forced through narrow places and generally made angry by the irregularities of the islands. Colonies of Atlantic grey seals basked on the rocks around almost every little bay. The Atlantic grey seal is one of the rarest of the world's seal species, more than half of which breed on the various outliers to the Outer Isles. North Rona, in particular, is a major breeding ground. Since 1914 the grey seal has been protected; before that date it had been hunted nearly to extinction. At the entrance to each bay, the entire colony swam out to meet us and escorted us past their territory, some coming within three or four feet of us. John produced a pair of goggles and capsized several times to observe them underwater. Borrowing his goggles, I did the same, entering a silent green world in which the seals twisted and turned and slid by with powerful, silent grace. I tried whistling underwater. Whether they heard anything or not, I don't know, but I felt some sense of communication with them as if they appreciated our attempts to meet them in their own element.

Passing two outcrops named The Eternal Isles, we arrived at Shillay and landed to inspect the deserted lighthouse. There used to be monks on Shillay who kept a beacon burning to warn ships of the dangerous reefs. Then, in 1864, the lighthouse was built. Nearly all the lighthouses in the western isles were designed and built by successive generations of the Stevenson family, of which

Robert Louis Stevenson, the author of *Treasure Island* and *Kidnapped* (amongst many others), was a member. The lighthouse was not locked, but all the windows were boarded up. We felt our way along the passage, hands sliding and fluttering along the wall, until we came to a gap – the start of the winding stone staircase to the top of the tower. I shall never forget that pitch black darkness. It is the only time I have experienced total absence of light. I could see absolutely nothing, not even a hand an inch in front of my face. Slowly we felt our way up the cold, musty, narrow twisting stairs. Now and then a step was missing, a space as black as all the rest of the blackness. What a relief to emerge into the daylight on the balcony below where the big lens and lamp once had been! The wind was rising and we were mindful of the thirteen or fourteen-mile crossing we had to make to John's home in Eochar at the north end of South Uist. But, for all that, we lingered. The five islands were spread out below us. These lone fragments of the Hebrides have something very special about them, at one and the same time an unspoilt innocence and an atmosphere that is ancient and mellow. Morton Boyd, the naturalist, says of the Monach Isles that their size is out of all proportion to their importance in the natural history of the British Isles. And I feel the same about their importance in the history of Robin Lloyd-Jones. All of us have a place or two in which we have left a part of ourselves, a treasure island. For me, this is one such place.

Chapter 11

Bleached Bones and Bothy Rats

Around South Uist

To circumnavigate South Uist clockwise, a round trip of about forty miles: that was the plan. John's house was on the water's edge at the northern end of the island. We were going to start and finish at his doorstep. I had flown to South Uist from Glasgow partly because it was quicker and I had a busy schedule that month, and partly because I couldn't face the thought of crossing the Minch in anything bigger than a kayak. For me, the terrors of sea-sickness in a lumbering, smelly ferry outweighed other considerations. As a result of this, I would have to use one of John's kayaks. My paddle I had brought with me, carrying it like a lance, ready to joust with the sea-dragons of the Hebrides. A paddle can become a very personal piece of equipment, the feel of the shaft in the hand, an exact knowledge of how much of your weight it will support in any given circumstance, the precise angle of the blade for a successful roll, the confidence that a tried and trusted friend brings. As we set out eastwards across the shallow green waters between South Uist and Benbecula, I adjusted to the borrowed kayak, to the feel of the cockpit and seat and the different way my knees and hips and thighs gripped it and controlled it, the subtle differences in its points of balance and centre of gravity, its characteristic responses to the various motions of the sea. At low tide the basin between Benbecula and South Uist becomes a vast sand flat. At Carnan there is an inn where travellers waited to ford the gap. Apparently, the lookout

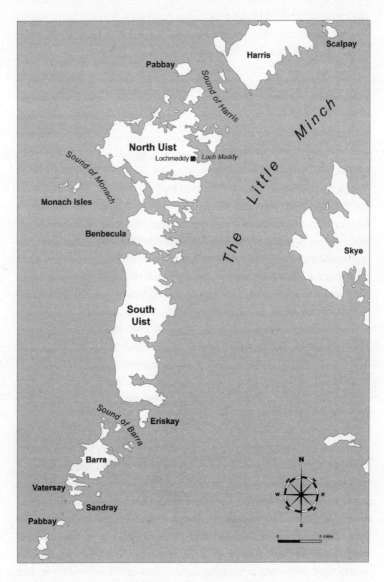

The Uists and the Monach Isles

posted to give a shout when the tide had fallen low enough for the crossing would often forget his duties and join in the revelry so that the crucial hour would be missed and then there would be nothing for it but to enjoy another twelve hours of drinking. There is no such convenient excuse these days, for a causeway and bridge have been built, under whose arches we shot, propelled by the outward rushing tide.

Four or five miles of rugged, barren coastline whizzed by until we put ashore near a little white cottage, where lived a relation of John's wife. In South Uist you cannot pass by the house of a relative without stopping to pay your respects – even if it's a kayak you're in.

The kitchen was a heady mixture of smells: paraffin, peat smoke, damp oilskins, tea-leaves and fish. We downed the obligatory 'wee dram' of whisky, the word 'wee' being somewhat of an understatement. On the water again, glowing internally, we paddled past scenery impressive in its loneliness, in its grey rocks and deserted moors. Turning a corner and taking a definite southerly course, we negotiated an inner passage, about half a mile long, between dark steep-sided rocks, at times squeezing through gaps hardly more than three or four feet wide, a route which would be impossible to almost any craft other than a kayak. Crossing the mouth of Loch Skipport, we encountered a stiff breeze blowing out of it, and the first smatterings of rain. On the far shore of the loch we rested beside a moored lobster boat. A cheery man in overalls and a woolly cap appeared from the cabin with a glass of whisky in each hand.

'A wee dram to see you on your way!' he exclaimed.

He told us, as he refilled our glasses, leaning over the side, that his lobster creels were being lifted by rival boats. 'Lobster rustling in the Wild Western Isles!' I thought . . . But I was on my third 'wee dram' by then. We paddled a not very straight line in grey, lumpy waters, under grey, drizzling skies.

'I know someone who runs an experimental mussel farm just along here,' John said. 'Shall we pay him a visit?'

'Will it mean another wee dram I can't refuse?'

'Yes, of course.'

I begged him to give this one a miss. Maybe the rain and the increasing wind and the fact that we still had a fierce headland to round had something to do with it, but my pleas were heard and we kept on course for Usinish Bay.

The landscape changed after Loch Skipport, rising to a ridge of hills which fell steeply into the Minch. Over these cliffs a series of waterfalls dropped into the sea. Some cascaded down the rock, spraying and sparkling, sporting rainbows like medal ribbons conferred upon them by the weak sun which was now breaking through; others plunged straight into the sea in a bubbling bombardment. If the overhang was pronounced, we were able to slip behind them into an entirely different world where the light shone through tumbling curtains whose permanence consisted of incessant change and renewal and where the thunder of falling water echoed from the cliffs. Some of the waterfalls were small enough to paddle into until they were directly overhead, drumming loudly on the hull, beating us on head and shoulder, driving bow or stern underwater with their force. For several miles we kept company with dark impending precipices made bright with sudden patches of green vegetation, passing from shadow into light and into shadow again, through waters which guzzled and snuffled amongst the roots of the cliffs and changed with startling abruptness from olive-green to blue-black or obsidian. We moved out of the leé of the cliffs to round the headland and lighthouse on Usinish Peninsula. The under-keeper of the lighthouse is quoted in some early account of the area as saying: 'No one realises how vicious midges can really be until you have been bitten by those of Ru Usinish.' I was telling John about our flight from the midges on the Garvellachs, but never finished the story because heaving seas off the headland suddenly demanded our full attention. After passing a stack known as Nicolson's Leap, in whose cracks baby fulmars sheltered, we ourselves found the shelter of Usinish Bay.

The Usinish bothy is a little stone hut with a mud floor and a corrugated iron roof, standing in some rather boggy moorland about a quarter of a mile from the beach. It is maintained by the Mountain Bothies Association. Until my visit to Usinish I had never heard of this organisation, founded in 1965, whose aim is 'to maintain simple unlocked shelters in remote country for use by walkers, climbers and other outdoor enthusiasts who love the wild and lonely places'. By way of thanks for the shelter we received in one of these wild and lonely places, I joined the association soon after this. Although I am not an active member who goes on weekend working parties, I hope that my modest annual subscription has perhaps mended a broken window or put a slate on a roof somewhere. To quote from *Mountain Days and Bothy Nights* by Dave Brown and Ian Mitchell:

> 'You use words like bothy, doss, howff – what's the difference?' asked one of the youths.
> 'A bothy's an auld hoose, like a cottage, that's become empty and is maintained as climbing accommodation. It comes from the old word for a farm-labourer's dwelling. A howff is a much simpler structure: a cave, a few rough boulders or a simple purpose-built shelter, like Slugan Howff.'
> 'Slugan Howff? What's that?'
> 'Oh, ye'll have to read the book to find out!' was the reply. 'And doss is just a word used to cover anywhere you sleep, be it bothy or howff.'

Thanks to a stiffish breeze, the midges were not out in force. We explored, admired misty views of Hecla and Beinn Mhor, saw a golden eagle wheeling high above the moorland, and then gathered driftwood from the stony beach and carried it up to the bothy. The same authors as quoted above, referring to Corrour Bothy, say: 'The benighted traveller need not starve at Corrour: he could make soup from the nourishing stock encrusted in the table's recesses.' This was certainly not true of Usinish bothy where everything had been left clean and tidy by previous occupants. With a wood fire roaring in the grate and our wet clothes on a line strung across the fireplace, we settled down to study the bothy's logbook. We appeared to be the only canoeists to make an entry in the log. There had been people on a Duke of Edinburgh Award scheme, sheep shearers, hill walkers, army cadets on a training exercise, and those simply in search of remote places – and not all were British by any means: there were German, New Zealand, Australian and Japanese entries. And nearly all of them, except the Japanese, had banged their heads on the low doorway. 'Is there a record for the number of times in a weekend?' someone wrote in the logbook. One group of Irish fishermen had used the book to advertise for girls to write to them, 'preferably rich girls'. There were recipes for a 'Benbecula Blaster' containing large measures of whisky, vodka and brandy; for limpet soup, for bothy stew, and several recipes for poisoning the bothy rat. The latter received frequent mentions: 'The bothy rat had half my supplies last night.' 'That blasted rat chewed a hole in my sock!' 'I stopped up the rat's hole with my gloves, but in the morning they were gone.' 'B.R. gnawed my chopsticks.'

In the margin opposite this last, rather illegible entry, was the comment, 'I can't read Chinese!' and it was signed 'Bothy Rat'.

Thereafter, Bothy Rat made regular comments. New and fiendish ways of getting rid of him were greeted with derision. 'Yah! Failed again!'

One particularly reflective and poetic piece started with the sentence, 'I have come here for the good of my soul' and then occupied several pages with soul-searching, self-doubt, and descriptions of the beauty of nature. In the margin was the ratty comment, 'If this is going to be the sort of drivel we get in the future, I'm leaving!'

He must have been mollified by a return to more prosaic comments such as, 'Baked beans for supper. Wind force eight during the night', for he was certainly still there and left tooth marks in my bar of salt-water soap. At least, since they didn't match John's teeth, I presume they belonged to Bothy Rat.

Rain drummed on the tin roof while we snuggled in the wooden bunks below. I recalled the foothills of the Himalayas and the deafening bombardment of massive hailstones on a similar roof. In the small hours of the morning, a party of four stomped in, stamping mud off themselves, shaking out wet clothing and arguing loudly about whose fault it was that they'd got lost. After another noisy hour of clattering pans and shining lights in our eyes, they settled down to sleep. Not long after, we were up and about in readiness to catch the tide which would take us down to Lochboisdale and round the southern end of the island. We were, if I remember rightly, unusually noisy in our preparations that morning.

I paddled on automatic control, still half asleep. A greyish damp morning, mist lifting and shredding across empty, denuded hills; a strong current disturbing the pattern of the waves as it wiffled out of Loch Eynort. In all this stretch of coast I did not notice a single habitation, a legacy of the clearances of the nineteenth century. Colonel John Gordon, who had bought South Uist and Barra, offered Barra to the nation as a convict station. The offer was not taken up, but Colonel Gordon was granted permission to transport the islanders to Canada. He landed police, bailiffs and press gangs on South Uist and had the local inhabitants dragged aboard his ship *Admiral*. Those who resisted were felled with truncheons and handcuffed. An eye-witness likened the scene to a slave hunt on the African coast. Nearly 2,000 people were cleared from South Uist in this manner and dumped on the inhospitable shores of Canada.

We debated whether it was worth going two miles out of our way to get hot coffee and bacon rolls at Lochboisdale, decided it wasn't and pressed on round the headland of Ru Melvick into the Sound of Eriskay.

This was where the ship the *Politician* foundered with 20,000 cases of whisky on board during the Second World War, an event which gave Compton Mackenzie the idea for his novel *Whisky Galore*, which was later made into a film. Eriskay is also the place where Bonnie Prince Charlie made his first landing on Scottish soil on 24th July 1745. *Scottish Island Hopping* describes Eriskay as 'a haven of tradition and individuality, an islander's island relatively unharmed by the uniformity of modern Britain.' Halfway through the sound we met a crofter in a rowing boat to which were tied two Highland cattle. They were swimming the mile and a half across the sound from Eriskay to South Uist. That has become an increasingly rare sight. These days you would be much more likely to meet a windsurfer in the sound. Barra, where a strong, steady wind from one direction or another can almost be guaranteed, has become a centre for the 'tigers' of the sport. This was the point at which we had to decide whether to continue up the west side of South Uist or opt for our escape route, which was to retreat into Lochboisdale and telephone for John's wife to come in the car and collect us. The Admiralty chart warns of heavy breakers in several places at the western end of the Sound of Eriskay and the *Sailing Directions* states:

> The western side of the Outer Hebrides is one of the most exposed coasts in Britain and an element of risk is necessarily associated with its navigation . . . It *must* be noted that if there is heavy westerly weather or if a westerly swell is running outside, *very heavy* and dangerous seas can be expected at the western end of all channels leading through to the west.

However, there was no heavy westerly weather, the sky was clearing, the wind was not rising. Ahead, there were plenty of white caps, but nothing actually terrifying. We pushed forward for the end of the sound and headed north. Eriskay, sad am I without thee.

But almost immediately I had a new love: the long west coast of South Uist. Such beauty is unforgettable. Keeping outside the belt of surf, in seas of emerald green, cobalt, lapis lazuli and turquoise, we paddled parallel to mile after mile of empty silver sands and green machair, behind which cumulus clouds billowed up and up. Sometimes the land was so low that the scattered white houses seemed to be floating on the sea. Several times we braved the surf to rest on a beach; and then it was hard to say which was more beautiful, the land viewed from the sea, or the wide Atlantic seen across a stretch of white sands.

In a bay with a Gaelic name like a salt wind sighing through sea grass, I heard the singing sands – millions upon millions of dry grains shifting in the wind, rustling and vibrating. I explored the machair. An ecstasy of wild flowers, solid splashes of colour, nearly all the types I had identified on the Monach Isles and others too: sea campion, marsh marigolds, poppies, tormentil, wild camomile. And everywhere there were birds: corn buntings, lapwings, plovers. My feet, scuffing through the sand, encountered a buried bone. I uncovered it and discovered more nearby. They must have been there for a number of years being scoured, bleached and polished. They belonged to a cow which either died in the dunes or was washed up in a storm. Precision instruments, marvels of skeletal engineering, and works of modern sculpture, wonderful to handle, to feel their hollows, curves, grooves and ridges, their subtle variations in texture. I filled a large bag with them. I have found few man-made works of art to rival them.

More paddling, fatigue banished by the sheer beauty of it all; another landing. Joy is a rise of gulls on a beach in Uist, where white dunes, green-topped, face green waves, white-capped; and skies of silver-grey touch grey-silver sands. Joy is the texture of sand beneath bare feet, soft and dry, sifting through the toes, corrugated, rippled and hard-ribbed, or wet and flatly slapping. Joy is a curving line, undulating dunes, a crescent of newly-wetted sand, marram grass bending to the wind, a curling wave. Harmony. The frilled edges of a scallop and the foam reaching up a beach; the rings inside an empty limpet shell and those of a tidal pool; grained driftwood and grained rock; and so many harmonies in white. It was a day for an awareness of the unity of things and for pondering on Blake's poem:

To see a World in a Grain of Sand
And Heaven in a Wild Flower,
Hold Infinity in the palm of your hand
And Eternity in an hour.

It was a day for lying on one's back and listening to the rhythms of the universe, to one's own heartbeat, to the ebbing of the tide; for sensing the spinning of the earth, the cycle of sea, cloud and rain, and of the seasons. I thought of the words of Rabindranath Tagore: 'The stream of life runs through my veins night and day, runs through the world and dances in rhythmic measure.'

I'm sure the Bothy Rat will be annoyed with me for saying so, but nowhere and at no time have I been more strongly aware of the cosmic dance than on South Uist.

Chapter 12

Towards the Land of the Ever Young

Kilchoan to the Treshnish Isles

On a summer morning four kayaks lifted their noses and headed south-west into a stiff breeze, the long bows thrusting into the oncoming sea. With me were Carol and Heather and Lofty, part of a group of sea canoeists from the north-east of England who were taking their holiday in Scottish waters. Push from the toes, through the body to the shoulder. My canoe was fully loaded, low in the water, less skittish than when an empty shell. Waves sluiced along the deck, parting either side of the cockpit. From Kilchoan on the Ardnamurchan Peninsula to the Treshnish Isles is twenty-five miles. A possible nine or ten hours of paddling lay ahead of us. We settled to a steady rhythm, body on automatic control, mind wandering free, grazing on cloud and wave.

Slowly a gap opened between the nearer cliffs and the white lighthouse of Ardnamurchan Point, a name which, freely interpreted from the Gaelic, means point of the high-sounding wave. Then the purple mountains of Rùm edged clear. Across the western horizon Coll and Tiree were merged into a thin indigo line, and over the port bow, Mull's northern coastline gradually enlarged and sharpened into focus.

All week it had been squally and the day had dawned with the weather in the same uncertain temper. Hourly we had listened to the shipping forecasts. The Treshnish Isles lie near the junction of sea areas Malin and Hebrides. We juggled with the two sets of figures and worried. We had stared at the high-altitude clouds, trying to decipher their long-term message. Several times we had climbed the hill behind Kilchoan Pier and estimated the wind strength from the white-capped waves beyond the headland. Possibly force four gusting to five. But would it increase? The coastline was inhospitable, with long stretches where an emergency landing would be difficult. A deterioration in the weather could have nasty consequences, not to mention being marooned indefinitely out on the islands. Finally we set off.

Approaching Mull's Caliach Point, we saw something moving on the waves, disappearing in the troughs, reappearing on the crests. Ten minutes later we drew level with two fellow canoeists. They were a middle-aged couple. With no previous experience of canoeing, each had given the other a brand new sea kayak for their twenty-fifth wedding anniversary and then set out to fulfil a long-held ambition to explore the west coast. They were glad of our company, I think, while we rounded the point, for suddenly the swell was bigger and the sea was coming at us from two directions at once. Strung out in the distance were the Treshnish Isles: little dark blue pimples rising from the sea. Lunga, in the middle of the chain, still ten miles away; beyond it the unmistakable outline of the Dutchman's cap. These eight islands and their skerries are eroded outliers of an ancient lava plateau.

Our two companions paddled on, heading for Calgary, while we turned into one of Mull's little cliffgirt bays for a late lunch. Jagged reefs barred the entrance, but the occasional larger wave rolled in, giving us a few inches' clearance. We passed from twilight fathoms to translucency, gliding over tide made lagoons of emerald and lapis lazuli and rippled sand seen through sapphires of splintered light. Our bows pushed aside soft forests of shining, reddish kelp. Grasping stems thicker than an arm we pulled ourselves over mucilaginous fronds. Stiff legs, slimy half-tide rocks, canoes heavy with camping gear . . . we slipped and cursed our way up the beach. Sandwiches, hot soup from a flask and the luxury of stretching and walking about. Raindrops speckled the smooth pebbles so that they resembled plovers' eggs.

Eyes glanced anxiously out to sea. The wind was veering and strengthening. The most exposed part of the crossing was still to come.

An hour later the tide was swirling and frothing round the little bay, inching up to the kayaks. We wriggled into our slender craft, fitted the waterproof apron over the cockpit rim and seal-launched off the seaweed-cushioned rocks straight into the water. An outgoing surge sucked us through the narrow entrance into the open sea. Next stop the Treshnish Isles.

Now the sea had a different motion, a rolling, surging rhythm that swelled beneath us, gathering us up, sweeping us on. Riding the crests, dipping and sliding into the troughs, with every wave a shift of balance, a quick adjustment of the blade. Over and over again, never the same, but all the time the underlying heart-beat of the ocean.

The *West Coast Pilot* had made no more than a passing reference to a tide-race off the north-east end of the Treshnish Isles, but then that worthy volume was written for sturdier vessels than ours. From a mile off we could see the race heaving and kicking and flecked with white breakers. We took a more easterly line than planned to avoid the worst of it. Even so, the seas were high and steep and curling at the top in a way that quickens the pulse.

It was at this point that my kayak sprang a leak. I had been experimenting with a bigger deck hatch in an attempt to make it easier to load gear into the narrow bows. If, for once, my bits and pieces had slipped through the hatch without difficulty, the sea was now doing the same! I must have taken in a hundredweight or more of water. Every time I sped down the steep front of a wave, the bows, instead of lifting again, continued on their down-ward trajectory. Several times I was submerged up to my chest before what little buoyancy there was asserted itself. I paddled flat-out for the nearest island. My kayak, glucking with internal waters, had developed a mind of its own. I was fighting hard just to keep on course. With much relief I made landfall on Cairn na Burgh More.

Meanwhile, Carol, Heather and Lofty continued round the island to see the ruins of Cairnburg Castle. In the twelfth and thirteenth centuries, when it guarded the main sea-lanes of the Lord of the Isles, it figured more prominently on charts than places like Glasgow or Dumbarton. Later, however, the saying, 'As busy as a sentry on Cairnburg' had somewhat sarcastic overtones. At one time, Maclean of Duart imprisoned his rival, Maclean of Lochbuie, in Cairnburg. To ensure the latter could leave no heir, Duart chose the ugliest hag he could find to act as gaoler, but, as W.H. Murray puts it, 'Lochbuie rose to the challenge and gave her a son.' When the others returned I told them about my difficulty in keeping a straight line.

'Now you know the true meaning of pig-headed,' said Lofty. He explained that sailing-ships used to load pig-iron as ballast. If too much was put in the bows, the ship would display the same obstinate tendencies that I had been contending with. We made the final push for Lunga, now only three miles off. This time my hatch was well sealed with double layers of waterproof repair tape.

Who has not felt the lure of the islands such as these? Uninhabited, isolated, each one small enough to give life simple, manageable proportions. And what better way to approach them than silently by kayak? John Fowles in his book *Islands* says: 'True islands always play the sirens' trick; they lure by challenging, by daring. Somewhere on them, one will become Crusoe again, one will discover something: the iron-bound chest, the jackpot, the outside chance ... the other great siren charm of islands is that they will not belong to any legal owner, but offer to become a part of all who tread and love them.'

And so it was with the Treshnish Isles.

We paddled past perpendicular black walls of lava. On the narrow ledges at their base, colonies of Atlantic grey seals haul out in October and November to complete their twelve-month cycle in which the birth of the pups is followed quickly by the next season. There is much yet to be learned about the grey seal colonies of the Treshnish Isles, but it is feared that many of the babies are swept to their deaths from the ledges by the Atlantic storms.

Our passage past Fladda and our approach to Lunga was marked by erupting colonies of sea-birds. They rose in clouds, circling suspiciously above us, shrieking and swooping, banking into blizzards of white under wing. The twenty-five species of sea-birds which breed regularly on the Treshnish Isles play a big part in maintaining the herb-rich pastures. In 1892 Harvie-Brown wrote of these islands: 'The whole short sweet pasturage, foot by foot, yard by yard, is manured by droppings of both quadrupeds and birds. We saw the effects of this rich manurage when visiting the islands in a later period of the seasons, when the cattle were eagerly feeding on full-grown herbage which almost completely hid from view the thickly lying manure.' There are no cattle now, but eighty to a hundred sheep graze the larger islands. The smaller islands have never been grazed and present an extremely interesting comparison, having completely different plant colonies, including some rare varieties of tall herbs.

The Treshnish Isles, too, are the winter quarters of up to a thousand barnacle geese. But this was summer, and it was the puffins, guillemots, razor bills, kittiwakes, fulmars, terns, cormorants and gulls that gave us noisy greeting.

In the lee of Lunga the water was quieter. We cruised past tiny Tigha Ogha – the House of the Mermaid. I remember one barren islet, cut off from Lunga by the tide, where a rabbit ran round and round . . .

Tired though we were, the magic of the islands filled us with a desire to circumnavigate Lunga before beaching our kayaks for the day. We rounded the southern cliffs, staring up at the clear-cut line between one lava flow and the next. On the exposed western side, the surf was thundering, daring us to try the inner passages between the cliffs and the offshore rocks. Adrenalin flowing, hearts pounding, we accepted the challenge. The Atlantic sweeps in, mounting the vanguard reefs and skerries; kayak swinging upwards on a tilting sea; swooping back on the outgoing surge. Where a thin hull had hovered seconds ago, glinting sea, cascading rock and gurgling emptiness. Survival is reading the waves aright. Survival is using the narrow zones between the breaking rollers and the chaos where waves hurl back from the cliffs into their own oncoming ranks. Survival is riding the close-walled channels on the exact moment between the ferocious backwash and the snarling approach of the next big breaker. The din of the surf is terrific, and the blood sings to its tune.

The rain-clouds of the afternoon had disappeared. It was a fine evening. Without unpacking our kayaks we hurried towards Cruachan, Lunga's 337-foot summit, to catch the last hours of daylight. Lunga is one and a quarter miles long and 600 yards wide at its broadest point. Like the other main islands it is quite treeless and covered in short, springy grass. The going would have been easy but for the continual dive-bombing of the gulls. Arms whirling, head turned, looking for the next attack, I fell into a small ravine. As I picked myself up, I wondered if the unusually large number of sheep's skeletons on the island might be due to gulls stampeding them over the cliffs, or is it simply that the predators which normally scatter the bones are absent here?

From the summit we could see the Paps of Jura forty miles to the south-east and the Cuillins of Skye sixty miles to the north. Looking westwards, with the sun sinking into the Atlantic behind Tiree, one could understand why the Norsemen bestowed the name Haubredey – the Isles on the edge of the Sea. And one could believe the legend of Tir Nan Og – the Land of the Ever Young, which lies west across the horizon.

Skirting the edge of a tall cliff, we looked down on steep-sided Dun Cruit, the harp-shaped rock in the sea. Its wild music was the noise of sea-birds in their thousands, the wind and the pounding of the Atlantic rollers. In the past, fishermen carried the masts of their skiffs up here to place across the chasm, thus gaining access to the birds and eggs on the outlying rock.

We prepared supper in the gloaming, beside the driftwood fire. I had packed dried food instead of tins by way of economising on weight. The trouble was, after my mishap with the hatch, they were no longer dry. I settled for porridge, always a good standby for canoeists, for it's one of the few foods which immersion in salt water actually improves. This was followed by several oranges, a fruit which comes in watertight containers far more efficient than any of my devising.

The others chose to bivouac in nearby caves. I pitched my tent beside the ruined houses whose rounded corners and dry-stone walls are not of this century. The last permanent inhabitants of the island left in 1824. They were Donald Campbell and his family. While shooting geese from his boat for the family pot, Donald was borne away to Coll by a squall. Such was the anxiety of his wife in the four days he was missing that, on his return, they decided to quit the island for ever. After that, the village was used only for temporary or seasonal shelter by fishermen and herdsmen.

Inside my sleeping bag I listened to the surf and the swash of wave on pebbled beach and recalled the words of John MacLintock. When describing the Treshnish anchorage, one of the most perfect in the Hebrides, he wrote in his book *West Coast Cruising:*

> To be really snug, let me be in the small cabin of a small yacht during heavy weather, and put between my boat and me and the leaping seas a small islet or two, just a few acres of sturdy rock, so that I may sit back in warm contentment and hear not only the whining rigging and the swishing rain, but also the loud thunders of the breakers round the corner. *That* is snugness.

For myself I would sacrifice snugness for something else: for a very special relationship with the sea, granted only to those who take her measure against their own puny strength.

Mice were rustling amongst the gear outside my tent. On St Kilda, the native mice disappeared after it was evacuated, probably because of competition from the more powerful field-mice. The latter are absent from Lunga and house-mice still live in and around the deserted village. Then eerie cries filled the darkness and strange voices babbled, sang and moaned. At the time, I did not know about the storm petrels which burrow underground, or occupy the ruins. Fraser Darling and J. Morton Boyd in their book *The Highlands and Islands* subsequently shed light on the matter for me. Referring to the ways of 'Mother Carey's chickens' they wrote: 'The churring noise in the stormie is one of the comforting things to the human visitor in his nights on a lonely island . . . the birds in the air have an arresting, wild staccato calling, but those in the burrows make an exceptionally sweet ascending trill, which is not often heard.'

Nor did I know of the habits of the Manx shearwater, whose cry is the stuff of nightmares, sounding like an unearthly shriek as of someone being throttled. Could the underground noises made by these birds be the origin of the Norse legends about trolls? An interesting correlation has been shown between the nesting sites of shear waters and place-names with 'troll' in them. Trollaval on Rùm, and Trollkarpin the Faeroes, for example, are both regular breeding places for shearwaters.

But, with no such explanation to steer my thoughts, they drifted towards treacherous whirlpools of imagination. I concentrated hard on that memorable sunset view from the summit. I began counting all the islands we had seen: Jura, Colonsay, Iona, Staffa, Ulva, Gometra, Bac Beag, Bac Mor . . . I had reached nineteen when I fell asleep.

Chapter 13

The Stolen Hours

Short excursions in the Clyde Estuary

At 4 a.m. the sun filters through my bedroom window and wakes me. I listen to the Clyde lapping at the lawn and the seabirds calling. I slide my kayak over the dewy grass into the pink dawn water. It glides across the glassy surface. Then, drifting, I hear the plop, plop of fish and watch the sunrise. Mackerel and sea-trout for breakfast, straight from the sea, cooked on a driftwood fire at Kilcreggan Point. Then home again, a shave and a shower and off to work. These hours, stolen from a day whose official schedule makes no such concessions, are very precious. They are an antidote to daily frustrations; they are a kind of mantra for serenity; they are to the average week what salt is to porridge. Like most people, after a hard day at the office, I find that a stiff something and tonic helps me unwind – my tonic is to paddle out to where tide-exposed sands are striping Craigendoran Bay with bars of gold, or to engage in a stiff tussle with wind and wave, round the buoy and back. At almost any seaside town along the coast of Britain it takes only ten minutes to escape from traffic, from other people, from noise and fumes – if you head straight outwards. To find similar peace and solitude on land, you may well have to drive for several hours. It is the instant escape in a kayak which is appealing. Five minutes after having the thought, I can be on the water. And in another five minutes I can find more than enough adventure and danger, if that is what I want. The Clyde Estuary may be ringed by built-up areas, but out in the middle, it can be as lonely and as frightening as the wildest and remotest of places. I am very lucky, of course, in that my house is on the shore. If I owned a yacht, on the other hand, it could take me anything up to an hour to rig and prepare it for sailing, not to mention the fact that I would probably have to drive to the place where the authorities had allocated me a mooring. I don't wish to deny the many pleasures of sailing, but it does seem to me that it is also accompanied by worries. When you own something that valuable, you wake up at night and listen to the wind howling and fret about whether the mooring is secure and the insurance policy paid up.

One fine summer morning, with a thick mist hanging over the water, I slipped from my bed and headed for the sandbars in mid-estuary which appear at low tide. I landed and stripped naked, running barefoot over the sand towards the low orange disc that was the mist-veiled sun. Unfortunately, in the mist, I had mistakenly landed on a spit joined to the mainland. A woman, up early to walk her dog, stared in surprise at the nude figure which materialised in front of her, then abruptly turned round and disappeared whence it came. Correcting my course, I again made a landing. Again I was mistaken. This time I was at the wrong end of the sandbar, the end which consisted of very soft mud. Too late. I had plunged into it and gone several reckless paces before I realised I was sinking deeper with every step. I was knee deep and still sinking. Every time I tried to extract one leg, the other sank even deeper. It took over half an hour of exhausting struggle to cover the ten yards back to my kayak. I was still naked. My legs, from the thighs downwards, were running with blood, slashed by razor-sharp mussels. I was thankful I hadn't sunk another six inches into the mud. My wife was still asleep when I returned home. After a shower, I slipped into bed beside her.

'You slept late this morning,' she said on waking. 'Mmmm,' I replied, but I knew I wouldn't get away with it for long.

And then there are the hours stolen not from the day but from the seasons. Winter days: bright cold days when the ice has to be emptied from the kayak before launching and when the snow-clad hills all around the sea lochs sing hallelujah; or days with dark, dramatic skies, with the water lit in patches through the clouds; days when hailstones rattle on the deck and make the sea jump and pop with white pearls. With the sun low in the sky, these are the rainbow months; rainbows which tinge the water and which can turn a flight of geese to green, blue and indigo. And early Spring, when the blossom and the snowflakes sprinkle my kayak in equal parts as I slide it across frosty grass; days when every headland around the bay is aflame with bright yellow gorse.

And hours stolen from the weather, the kind of days when the steamer trips are cancelled, when there is not a sail in sight. These are the days to put on a wet-suit and go out with no other intention than of sporting with the waves, of getting wet and of returning to a long hot bath. Or the days when it's raining jugfuls (as they say in Spanish), when golfers and cricketers opt for the clubhouse. There's a fascination in being at the very point of the hissing fusion between two elements, where the sky merges with the sea and makes a million craters a second upon its surface. From upside-down, looking up, the dance of the raindrops is a beautiful sight – and you're hardly any wetter that way round!

The hours stolen from the night are amongst the most magical of all. Calm, moonlit nights with twinkling lights circling the coast, the buoys and beacons flashing their guiding messages and the moon continually laying a silver carpet in front of me; clouds racing past the moon.

> 'The moon was a ghostly galleon tossed upon cloudy seas'
> *The Highwayman* by Alfred Noyes

Drifting in a Milky Way. Stargazing. The Great Bear, Cassiopeia, Cepheus, the Herdsman, the Pleiades. Constellations in the sky, mankind's oldest picture book.

All over Scotland, on June 24th, hill walkers and mountaineers gather on peaks at midnight to mark the occasion of the

longest day in the year. And canoeists have their own rites . . .
weather permitting. It is surprising how many midsummer nights
feel more like midwinter. Since ancient times, fire festivals have
been held all over Europe at the summer solstice. As Sir James
Frazer puts it in *The Golden Bough:* 'The summer solstice, or
Midsummer Day, is the great turning point in the sun's career,
when after climbing higher and higher day by day in the sky, the
luminary stops and thenceforth retraces his steps down the heav-
enly road. Such a moment could not but be regarded with anxiety by primitive man.'

According to a medieval writer, the three great features of the
midsummer celebration were the bonfires, the procession with
torches round the fields, and the custom of rolling a wheel, all of
which are metaphors for the sun and its path through the
heavens.

At about nine o'clock at night, in what seemed like full
daylight, except that there was a greenish tinge to the sky, we
began towing rafts of driftwood out to an exposed mud flat in
the Clyde. There were twelve of us, sea canoeists from all around
the area. Already the tide was reclaiming the mud flat, By the
time we had built and lit the bonfire on the most elevated and
firmest part of the temporary island, our kayaks, drawn up in a
circle around it, had been found by the searching fingers of the
tide and were starting to float. We took to our kayaks, switching
on the lamps fixed around our heads – not quite the same as
holding aloft a burning brand, but the practical difficulties
involved in this were too great. Slowly we circled the fire with
long, deliberate strokes, feeling its heat on our faces, gliding
through molten gold. It was midnight. We stopped paddling. A
bottle of whisky was tossed from one to the other round the
circle. The sky had darkened, but even without the light from the
fire, one could have read a newspaper out there. A breeze sprang
up. The fire roared and flared, sending sparks across the water.
As the tide tightened its grip on the diminishing island and
touched the red-hot embers, the fire hissed and spat like some

angry sea-serpent and threw up clouds of steam. Then, amidst explosions and mighty eruptions, the glowing, pulsating pyramid collapsed and was extinguished.

On another Midsummer Night, when there were only four of us, and the weather forecast was on the pessimistic side, I finally found the answer as to what to do with my old kayak, the one with a wooden frame and a skin stretched over it. It was beyond use, yet I hadn't wanted to dispose of it. On it I painted emblems of the sun, then I stuffed it with straw soaked in paraffin and towed it out to sea. Somewhere off Cloch Point Lighthouse, in a choppy sea, we set fire to it and let it loose. We followed the burning vessel, not sure whether we were Drake's sea dogs, Vikings or ancient druids, but each finding a meaning to what we were doing.

As I write this, it is a fine April night, the stars are out, the moon is rising over the hills, mermaids are singing on a distant sandbank . . .

Chapter 14

Here Sea Monsters and Sundry Miracles Abound

An excursion up Loch Long

When the Helensburgh clock struck six, I was already afloat. Sea and sky, vertical and horizontal, gently merged their imperceptible qualities of grey. The paddle's dip and thrust seemed muffled by the mist as my bows probed seawards, away from the embracing arms of the bay and the dreaming town which quietly pulled a sheet around itself and slumbered on. I steered towards a red cone, some ten feet in the air and about twenty yards away, probably the top of a racing buoy, and immediately bumped against it – a floating beer can. Somewhere – behind me, in front of me, to my left, to my right? – a dog was barking and, in the distance, a foghorn mourned. I drifted on a surface of polished steel imagining myself to be a figure in a silver-bromide print, till rods of jet slanted across my reverie, emanating from an unseen ship and destined to wash upon an unseen shore. Paddling again, breath hissing, mist and sweat mingling on the face. A beetle ran from side to side across my deck. Back and forth, back and . . . ghosting towards me was the same red cone – the same beer can – I had bumped ten minutes ago! While drifting, I must have revolved without realising it. Either that, or I was travelling in circles. Having arrogantly assumed that a compass was unnecessary in my own home waters, I was without means of navigation. Well, almost – lurking in the pocket of my life jacket was a mouldy sandwich. By continually casting my bread upon the waters and observing the tidal drift, I navigated towards Kilcreggan Point and the mouth of Loch Long. A fragment of chart floated by. I scooped it from the water and studied its intricate patterns of inlets, channels and lakes. Diamond Island, Poverty Point, Deer Ranger Light, Triumph, Quarantine Bay, Homeplace. Trimmed and ironed flat, the chart is now mounted on my study wall. For as long as I refrain from finding out where it is, it will remain a treasure map for the imagination, a place where fabulous happenings are possible – but right here, in the Clyde Estuary, a monster was rearing up in front of me, 200 feet high.

No oil rig had stood there yesterday. It must have been towed into place late last evening to await its final fitting out. I crept between massive legs around which currents sucked and guzzled, into an underworld of dark upwellings. Above me, millions of tons of steel throbbed and hummed and clanged with hollow echoes. Tilting my head I gazed straight up into the drilling-shaft. The sky revolved, a swell swept in, unleashing a chaos of slapping, exploding sea. Simultaneously, a jet of scalding water issued from a pipe high overhead, drilling the water uncomfortably close to my bows. I backed out, banging hard against a vast limb of steel.

As the rig softened at the edges and dissolved, I met a man walking on the water – a fisherman standing far out on a submerged spit. As he, too, faded into the mist, I saw my second monster of the day. The pointed reptilian head, the serpentine humps, they were unmistakable – and wasn't Loch Long, one of the deepest sea lochs in Western Europe, only a few miles away? Then one hump after another changed shape as the feeding ducklings raised their heads and followed their mother in a quacking line.

Soon after this, I overtook a becalmed yacht, its sails empty of wind. We exchanged a wave and a cheery word. I remembered the challenge I had thought of issuing to the local sailing club . . . but had not done so and probably never will. It is my contention that, if a kayak were to race a sailing dinghy over a circular course of about two miles, for seven days in succession, the kayak would most probably win the series. The likelihood is that for two of the days the weather would be too rough for the dinghy, but not for the kayak; for another two days it would be too calm for sailing; the remaining three days the dinghy would probably win, even though it would have to make a zig-zag tack on at least one of the legs.

Slowly the mist dispersed, revealing bruised skies and a seascape infinitely varied in tone and texture: lakes of Indian ink, obsidian pools, mirrors of silvered glass splintering in light breezes. I glided through mushroom fields of cloud which each paddle-dip multiplied, and, dreaming limbo-dreams, slid through shoals of waxing suns.

My friend the beetle returned from the known limits of the New World, that is to say, from the extent of my bows. A mile ahead, the breeze was chopping up the smooth surface. Soon waves would be sluicing along the narrow deck and beetle would be washed overboard. A rest, a bar of chocolate, then, fashioning a paper boat from the wrapper, I put beetle aboard. He waved from the stern as his brave little craft headed for the nearest land.

The paddle steamer the *Waverley* churned past me, its deck crowded with day-trippers bound for Rothesay. It is the last sea-going paddle steamer in the world to be in operation. As I hitched a lift on its wash, I reflected on the decline of the steamers and of the habit of thousands of Glaswegians of going 'doon the watter' on a pleasure cruise. Before World War I there were some forty vessels plying to and from the Clyde resorts. Rothesay was the Charing Cross of the Clyde and there might be four or five steamers at the pier at any one moment; and, in the Clyde Estuary, it would not be unusual for fifteen or more steamers to be within sight of each other. The competition was intense, with no fewer than nine different companies vying with each other for the passenger trade. Several companies were on the same run and shared the same piers. They would race each other to the piers to get the biggest share of passengers. Most of these earlier boats had cheap and ineffectual boilers which belched out 'reek' to such an extent that passengers used umbrellas to protect their clothes from falling soot. The communal singing on these boats, accompanied by a German band, was a great feature of such outings. On summer evenings, there would be music all over the water for miles around. By the 1950s there were only about eighteen steamers operating, of which the best known were the *Waverley*, the *Jeanie Deans*, the *Duchess of Hamilton* and the *Jupiter*. By the 1960s the steamers were fast disappearing. Increasing affluence meant that more Glaswegians went to Spain for their holiday rather than to Clyde coast resorts and more families owned a car; besides which, the rising costs of fuel were making the steamers uneconomic to run. Now, more than fifty piers lie abandoned.

Blue skies were breaking through when I reached the wide opening to Loch Long. Here, with the wind giving motion to the sea, my third monster and my second miracle of the day occurred in quick succession. A thick white serpent, thirty or forty feet long, wound through the water towards me. Then a hand emerged from the depths and beckoned. The first, the distorted reflection of a jet plane's vapour trail. The second, a discarded heavy industrial glove, bobbing upright in the waves. And it was not fire raging across the hills, but mist escaping from the thickly wooded slopes.

The sea rolled down the loch at a lively pace, each wave gathering below my thighs like a horse bunching for the gallop. Revelling in the motion, I sped joyously towards the purple silhouettes of Ben Vorlich, Ben Arthur and Ben Narnain, while beyond their jagged ridges armadas of cloud sailed in from the west. Via headphones and cassette, Mozart rolled through my head, magically at one with the rhythm of the sea and the billowing, upward-building clouds. The wind herding white breakers down the loch, sheep on the hills; the curving arc of a white wing, the crescent of Spring snow on Beinn Ime – the world was in harmony, ever moving, ever-changing, beautiful harmony.

Fffsswash! The glistening black shape of a porpoise arched through the air beside me, then plunged. Whoosh! Shakily I removed the headphones and paddled more slowly, tensed for the next rising. Whoosh! I jerked round. With an explosive expulsion of air, it cleared the waves parallel to my kayak, its eye rolling sideways to look at me, the spray from its re-entry wetting me. I waited. There it was! Curving, weaving, bouncing straight at me! It dived underneath me, bursting upwards on the other side. The game continued for a good ten minutes, he enjoying himself immensely, and I, pleased to be accepted as a fellow creature of the sea, but apprehensive lest he become too boisterous. What would he have thought of me, I wondered, if I had been wearing my wet-suit of shiny black neoprene? With a mighty leap and a splash that rocked the kayak he was gone. Even though I sent out telepathic messages that he was definitely not included in my monster count, he did not return.

Three miles further down the loch, when I did see my fourth monster of the day, it was of a much more deadly species, a nuclear submarine, stationary on the surface. Around it circled a spotter ship, its radar antennae gyrating. The leviathan and its pilot fish lay between me and the landing place I had selected for my lunch-break. Probably because I was so low in the water and in the troughs for at least half the time, I penetrated the circle undetected. I aimed to clear the submarine by about thirty yards. However, as I drew near, a klaxon blared, marines armed with sub machine guns poured out of a hatch, jumped into a rubber dinghy and roared towards me. I gave them a cheery wave and enquired as to the time of day. I was in danger, explained the young lieutenant. If the submarine were to dive, I could be in all sorts of bother. And, by the way, was that bulge in my pocket a camera by any chance? And what was my name and address? We parted with exchanges of civility and I paddled off at a smart pace, my spine tingling with the feeling of being watched. No doubt, at that very moment, a security check on me was underway. When I next looked round the submarine was gone. Changed days from when the Viking longships marauded up this loch.

My chosen place on this beautifully wooded, uninhabited shore was sheltered from the wind. After consuming soup and sandwiches, I stripped and lay on the salt-kissed, warm, wave-rounded rock.

As soon as I opened my eyes I knew I had slept too long. I dressed hurriedly, packed the canoe, launched and set out on the return journey. This time I kept close in-shore, skimming past beech and larch which proliferated amongst tumbled rocks, past giant clumps of wild rhododendrons and close-packed forestry plantations of spruce in whose branches herons nested. The steep slope plunged straight into the loch with no intervening shelf. Carved slabs of schist and quartz slipping into a pellucid zone, palely shining like amber, onyx, carnelian or jade. Mile after mile I slid past the ancient, ice-chiselled, sea-smoothed bones of the earth, every inch a marvel of grain and texture. And, over these time-etched rocks, in delicate shades of pink, white and grey, lichens spread their grotesque and fantastic shapes. The finest galleries of modern art in the world could not have produced an exhibition to rival these works of nature.

My pace was slowing. Since leaving Helensburgh twelve hours ago, I had covered more than thirty miles. I pushed on to make the most of the remaining light. Glen Finart and Ardentinny seemed a long, long time in the passing. Wearily, but with a Haydn violin concerto lifting my heart, I paddled through the dying embers of the day. When Greenock, Gourock and Dunoon shimmered like diamond bracelets and the Cloch Point Lighthouse was blinking steadily, I nosed into a small inlet and thankfully eased myself out of the narrow cockpit. Surrounded by stranded tree trunks which had been stripped and smoothed by the sea until they resembled moon-bathing beasts from outer space, I ate my sandwiches toasted on a driftwood fire.

The sea was restless beyond the little bay and a spread of dark wings hid a new-hatched moon. On rounding a point, I was greeted by a new galaxy of lights – a bright cluster that was the oil rig, another that was . . . I knew this home stretch so well, yet I was confused. Lights were not where they should be. Was it banks of mist or unseen headlands breaking the expected pattern? Or was I looking at a different stretch of coast? And which was reflection and which was not? And which . . . the dark, cold waters reached up for me and closed over my head. I hung upside-down, disorientated. Gasping, I rolled upright. Had I fallen asleep? Had an invisible wash taken me unawares?

I moved closer to the shore. Dark undergrowth murmured and rustled as I swished by. Then something huge and monstrous broke the surface, flailing the water and screeching horribly. I nearly capsized a second time from sheer fright. A panic of wings churned the water and flapped heavily into the air – gulls. They had been resting on the spit where I'd met the man walking on the water. The spit marked the point where I must leave the shore and head out across open water for Helensburgh. The breeze had strengthened, the sea was higher, steeper, faster. To be buffeted by waves you cannot see or anticipate is an unnerving experience, doubly so when you're alone.

At last my hull grounded on the Helensburgh shore. I carried my kayak through the shallows towards houses from which the night had been banished by drawn curtains. A man exercising his dog on the beach seemed startled when I walked out of the sea. I stood there, dripping, and assured him that there was nothing like a quiet day on the water.

Chapter 15

A Born-again Canoeist

Loch Long – Sound of Scarba – Firth of Lorn

For a couple of years canoeing fell by the wayside. Mostly it was pressure of work, another book on the way and the lack of companions with whom to canoe regularly, but it was also because a rival had appeared on the scene: windsurfing. There would be the odd trip around the bay in my kayak, particularly on windless days, but no big expeditions, not until I'd mastered that board and sail. No man can serve two masters. It was at this time that Michael, a hill walking friend and colleague at work, expressed an interest in sea kayaking. Once my love-hate relationship with windsurfing had reached a more even keel, so to speak, I began regular sessions with Michael, who was a complete beginner at canoeing. Instructing Michael was just what I needed. I had grown slack, my skills were adequate but not as sharp as they had been; even before my desertion to windsurfing, I had stopped practising my strokes; I hadn't bothered to keep my rolling technique in good order; I was growing careless and complacent in my approach to expeditions. In fact, I was well on the way to being 'an accident waiting to happen'. But now I had to demonstrate, to set an example, to analyse and discuss what I did, be responsible again. After a week or two, Michael was ready to learn the rescue drills. In order that he might rescue me, I did a deliberate capsize, the first I had done in a long time. As my head went under, the thought occurred to me that this was like a baptism and that my canoeing was taking on a new lease of life.

'I'm born again!' I shouted as I surfaced.

'First you're meant to be saved,' Michael said, moving in to perform the drill I'd shown him.

Standing on my lawn with Michael, preparing for an evening session on the water, I took stock of the many changes in my equipment and clothing since the day that Archie and I had launched our kayaks for the first time from this very spot. The biggest change was that I now had a new sea kayak, not a home-made effort, but one professionally made to a Derek Hutchinson design, with watertight compartments and hatches and an adjustable bar for a foot-rest. What a joy to have a kayak that didn't leak and from which I could emerge still dry! My paddle was different, too. After the first couple of years of paddling with a standard-length paddle and shape of blade, I had been converted to the long, thin Eskimo-type blade and a longer shaft, both of which, in my opinion, are less tiring to use when paddling long distances. The latter gives more leverage and support and a bigger arc when executing a turning sweep-stroke; the former, the long blade, slips into the water a bit at a time and distributes the energy put into each stroke more gradually, compared to a spoon blade which grabs the water in one big bite, requiring eighty per cent of the effort all at once. A neoprene spray deck had replaced the nylon one, the main reason for this being that it was more waterproof, warmer and more tight-fitting, which meant it wouldn't get pushed in by a heavy sea breaking over it and it was less likely to come off accidentally when rolling. Instead of shorts and old tennis shoes, I now wore a waterproof overall and welly boots. Although I always have a wet-suit in the kayak, I don't wear it unless the conditions absolutely demand it, preferring the freedom and better ventilation of looser clothing. My old life jacket which fitted over the head had given way to a waistcoat style of jacket. I prefer this type, not only because I find it more comfortable, but also because it gives more protec-tion to the ribs and vital organs in the event of being rammed by pointed bows or bashed against rocks. And much more attention was given to keeping my gear dry. Gone were the days of expecting fragile bin bags to do the job properly. I consider an investment in rubberised or PVC bags with special waterproof fastenings to be well worth the money. What else? Lots of little things, like: I now carried windproof and waterproof lifeboat matches; and I protected my thermos flask (having broken at least three) by putting it inside the cut-off sleeve of an old wet-suit. Another thing was different: my attitude to being immersed in the cold sea. Before I started windsurfing, a deliberate capsize was something I contemplated with a certain dread and loathing, but falling into the Clyde had now become such a commonplace event that the old reluctance had almost disappeared.

'How do you withstand the pressures of work so well?' a colleague recently asked me, twitching nervously as he lit a cigarette with a shaky hand.

'I owe it all to windsurfing and canoeing,' I replied. 'As the cold waters of the Clyde close over my head, I suddenly see all my other troubles in their true perspective.'

The born-again canoeist sees with new eyes. In fact, it was Michael's eyes which gave me a fresh view of things. Through him I relived the thrill of renewing my affair with the sea, with the Scottish west coast, with everything to do with sea kayaking.

I discovered again the delights of routes I knew too well, simple joys I had grown used to. 'It's like falling in love again,' I said to Michael. 'Don't even mention it.' 'Love?'

'No, falling in!'

Occasionally, Michael would apologise because he thought he might be going too slowly for me, or cramping my style in some way, but I have always considered that the exchange of my experience for a virgin vision pregnant with wonder (as the saying goes) was more than fair. Actually, what I gave in exchange was more than mere experience, it was priceless knowledge, The Secret Of Successful Canoeing. According to *The Hitchhikers' Guide to the Galaxy,* the answer to the Meaning of Life and Everything is

42; well, the Secret of Successful Canoeing is porridge. Porridge carried in a thermos flask, with tinned milk and masses of brown sugar, has been known to calm raging storms, to warm cold days, to make long voyages shrink by several miles, to give courage to lions and brains to scarecrows.

'I thought the Meaning of Life was 64,' Michael said.

'No, it's definitely 42.'

'No wonder I've been going wrong.'

Of all the various training outings, there are three about which Michael still speaks with a kind of reverence. One was the trip down the western shores of Loch Long (unlike another time I went that way, we drove rather than paddled to the entrance to the loch). To find a roadless wilderness so close to the conurbations of the Clyde, and yet so accessible in a small boat, is some kind of minor miracle in itself; that it should be so beautiful – the variety of trees, the lichen-covered rocks, the cormorants, the rhododendrons, the mountain vistas up and down the loch – is exhibiting strong forty-two-ish tendencies. Part of this same trip was a stop at Carraig nan Ron, an island rock at the end of the rugged peninsula known ironically as 'Argyll's Bowling Green', which separates Loch Goil and Loch Long. A miniature island with a miniature lighthouse. There was something about its shape, its smallness, the whiteness of the beacon, its position at the junction of the lochs – I'm not sure what it was, but there was and always has been a compelling quality about that place; I find it almost impossible to pass it by. An oyster catcher was nesting on it. It circled the rock, waiting for us to leave. We were worried that it might abandon the two eggs altogether if we disturbed it for too long, so, after cutting short our stay, we continued on our way.

Loch Goil. Seldom have I moved so fast in a kayak as on the wind-assisted five miles up the length of the loch to Lochgoilhead; and seldom have I slogged into a wind for so little result as I did on the return journey. The wind must have been force eight, gusting to nine, possibly even stronger in short bursts as it funnelled between the hills on either side of the loch. I don't remember the waves being particularly big, but the sheer weight of the wind I do remember: it pressed against the chest, it snatched at the paddle blades, it threatened to knock the kayaks over with its force. Michael told me later that he'd been a bit depressed and that he'd 'got a tremendous lift' from that trip. With a wind like that, he was lucky not to have taken off right over the mountains.

Down the Sound of Jura. A mountain-lined aisle with a blue-veiled Ireland waiting at the end, like a bride at the altar. Jura hidden behind vertical grey-brown palisades of rain which slowly advance across the Sound towards us. On my right-hand side it is raining, heavy drops bombarding the water only inches from my kayak; on my other side it is not raining. I am paddling in the sunshine, while Michael, only a few yards to my right, is paddling in the rain.

'I think the gods are trying to tell you something, Michael. They're saying you should be a clean-living lad like me.'

The expedition we'd been building up to was to the area off Easdale. This was much the same water that Archie and I had covered on our first big trip. Needless to say, Michael had to hear all the stories from that first time, the waitress, the ex-teacher, storm-bound on Belnahua, etc. The plan was different this time, though. We were camping in style at Easdale in a tent in which you could actually stand up, and doing three day trips from that base. The first day was Belnahua revisited. On the black slate beach of Belnahua was a bottle tied to a little wooden raft. In the bottle was a message from a German woman. It said: 'Please add your name and address to this paper; say where you found it and give the date; then send the bottle on its way again. The sea unites us all.' The bottle had started its voyage at the Mull of Galloway nine months before. There were two other names below the first one: a young girl (judging by her writing) who added her name near her home town of Portpatrick, and an English tourist who found the bottle on Gigha. We added our own names and details and set it adrift. I often wonder if that bottle is still afloat, and where it is now, and how many people it has united, even if they never knew it.

On the second day we went through the Sound of Scarba. Grey mists rendered the coast barely visible. With Michael, I marvelled anew at the power of the current which was carrying us south. I thought about the message in the bottle. 'The sea unites us all.' Yes, in so many different ways. It flows through time, uniting me with people long dead. This same current had run century after century, behaving in the same predictable way, to the hour, to the minute, changing the direction of its flow exactly on time according to moon and sun for thousands of years; men in coracles would have known precisely the times of its movements and made use of them, so would the Norsemen and all the seafaring folk after them, and so did we.

In the Grey Dog, the narrow strait between Lunga and Scarba, an otter was playing in the last of the ebb tide. We watched, impressed both by the strength of the current and the agility of the otter. Continuing our ride on the southward galloping main-stream, I told Michael more about the Corryvreckan.

'We'll just poke a nose into the entrance, but no more than that,' I said.

We paddled on, expecting to see the gap between Jura and Scarba open up any minute, catching faint glimpses of some distant shore to our left, speculating about exactly which part of the mainland it was. We paddled some more and still the entrance to the Corryvreckan did not appear. Surely we couldn't have passed by it and not seen it in the mist? Low cliffs lined the near bank. Where were we? I began to feel uneasy. The glimpses of coastline didn't quite fit together like they should if we were where we ought to be. A tiny inlet opened up. We dodged into it, our kayaks rumbling and bumping over big, smooth pebbles. Momentarily our concern over our whereabouts was dispelled by the beauty of this tiny beach like a nest filled with giant china eggs, each one so smooth and rounded; an Aladdin's cove glistening with natural treasure. Then, with furrowed brows, we consulted maps. The mist lifted for an instant revealing the far shore. Oh my God! If it was that close, it couldn't be anything else but the Jura shore of the Corryvreckan! We were right in the middle of it! We had followed the Scarba coastline, its westward curve being so gradual that we hadn't noticed the change of direction. It was the low water slack, before the flood tide started. For the moment, nothing stirred out there. Luckily for us, it was Neap tide and not Spring tide, which meant that there was a total of half an hour of slack, of which about ten minutes had elapsed.

'Let's get the hell out of here!' I said. 'In another twenty minutes this place is going to be a raging torrent.'

We had been paddling for about five minutes when we spotted another little cove which we'd missed on the way in. Three canoeists were squatting beside their kayaks having a brew-up. They motioned us in, inviting us to join them in a cuppa.

'Time for a quick one,' I said, thinking that I could, very subtly, find out where we were. 'It'd be unfriendly to refuse.'

'And we can ask them where we are.'

'The thought never crossed my mind. I mean, it's not as if we're lost. Not really lost.'

The three young men were from the Newcastle area. We drank their tea and chatted about sea-canoeists we knew in common, and about what they were planning to do during their week on the west coast of Scotland.

'More tea?' asked one of our hosts.

'Exactly which bay is this?' I asked casually, unfolding the map and holding out my cup.

A horny finger indicated a point on the Scarba shore bank opposite to where the Corryvreckan whirlpool develops. The tea was a fresh brew, too hot to knock back in one gulp. It would be rude to leave it. We sipped and blew and sucked, trying to down it as quickly as possible. With words of thanks, we sauntered nonchalantly towards our kayaks, breaking into a panic-stricken run halfway there. Launching as fast as we could, we paddled like mad towards the exit from this death trap. The water was starting to stir and heave, but nothing too alarming. Our pace slackened.

'Phew! I was worried for a moment back there,' Michael said.

Then, all of a sudden, the current pounced, was accelerating round a promontory, pouring into the gulf, gathering strength by the second. Our stroke-rate doubled . . . then trebled . . . but we were moving backwards. Behind us the water was seething, rising up in ugly welts, kicking and roaring. I managed to edge over closer to the shore where I knew a counter-current would assist our escape. Michael, who was wearing his wet-suit, was definitely overheating, bright red in the face, looking distinctly distressed as he was carried inexorably back into the gulf.

'Move over this way! To the side!' I yelled above the terrifying roar.

Michael heard me, did it, and was making forward progress.

'What price a cup of tea?' I commented, as we recovered in a little bay, clear at last of the pull of the current.

The return to Easdale was via Cuan Sound, the narrow channel about one mile long which connects the Firth of Lorn with Loch Melfort. A strong tide was running through it, going our way. Compared to the horror from which we had escaped, it was like a friendly babbling brook. The last stretch was done in thickening mist. I set a compass bearing, trying to allow for the extent to which the swell and the tide would keep pushing us off course. An hour later I began to worry. According to my calculations, if we were paddling at about four knots, Easdale harbour should be coming into sight. Nothing was visible. Nothing but white shrouds. Almost imperceptibly, the mist thinned, giving the merest hint of grey hills. They seemed so distant; it must be the coast of Mull. Had we passed Easdale without knowing it? Then the shrouds twitched aside and there was Easdale right in front of us, the entrance to the harbour less than 100 yards away.

* * *

Our third and last day was clear and bright. We ventured north-wards on a spanking sea into the Firth of Lorn, outflanking Insh Island and landing on Eilean Duin. A lush, verdant island, rich with wetland vegetation untouched by drainage, by cultivation or by sheep; dense, difficult to move through, a reminder of how things were long ago, impressive in its extravagant abundance. I recalled the words of Robert Aitkinson in his book *Island Going:*

> It has never seemed reasonable to me that the west coast of Scotland, so rugged and peat-ridden, should also be in charac-ter with a dripping proliferation of vegetation as rank and strong as on a sewage farm. The ideals of the vegetable king-dom must be far from those of warm-blooded creation;what passes for mildness to a herb is to sentient beings raw and searching seaside chill.

We squelched and struggled to the top-most point of the island to admire the view of water, mountains and islands in every direction. In a delightful account of a canoe trip made in 1885, entitled 'Watery Wanderings Mid Western Lochs', there is a description of this same view:

> I have looked long and wonderingly at many a scene. From the pine-crested mountains across the valley of the Great Salt Lake, and from heights along the banks of many of the American rivers; from the mountains of Wales and Western Ireland; across the wonderful Vale of Gloucestershire, and from fifty other well-known vantage spots in all parts of this my native land; but nothing so vanquished my susceptibility to admire nature in her naked truth and rugged dignity as this impressive Firth of Lorn.

Our lunch was not quite as grand as that of the author and his companions. Somehow, they always seemed to have room in their canoes for hampers containing whole chickens, bottles of wine, pheasant pie, knives and forks, cooked fruit and 'a few similar etceteras'. My Marmite sandwiches tasted good in the fresh air, all the same. While we ate, our eyes were drawn again and again to the south coast of Mull and its miles of cliffs, to the grandeur of Ben More and to the long beckoning finger of the Sound of Mull.

'Next time,' we said. 'The next time we can get away, that's the place for us.'

Chapter 16
Mull Broth

Along the south coast of Mull

One Saturday morning in September, two zombies paddled out of the Sound of Kerrera, their minds tucked up in bed, their bodies protesting at the 4 a.m. rise and the long drive. With our muscles still adjusting to the weight of the fully loaded kayaks, we passed the crumbling ramparts of Gylen Castle on the lonely southern end of Kerrera Island. Grey castle, grey sea, grey sky. Ahead of us an eight-mile crossing to Duart Point on the island of Mull. This being near the end of a season's paddling, we reckoned we qualified as 'hardened sea-gull eating' paddlers who could average between three and four knots per hour. Even allowing for the fact that the ebb tide in the Firth of Lorn would continually push us off target, I calculated that the crossing should not take much more than two hours. Our plan was to reach Duart Point at 'the bottom right hand corner of Mull' while the ebb tide still had enough power to squirt us north-westwards up the Sound of Mull, the channel which separates the island from the wilds of Morven. On the last small island before the main crossing began, we stopped for a late breakfast, or perhaps it was a second breakfast, our kayaks sliding and scraping up a narrow gutter as, simultaneously, four or five seals slithered off the island and took to the water, their dark eyes reproaching us. An island of rock pools, each one a life-filled world of its own, some bright, bright green with plants and bordered by big sea-daisies, others like chalices brimming with cloud and sky. As

we were leaving, Michael tried to bridge the gap between the
rock and his kayak by sitting on his paddle. There was a cracking
sound and the wooden shaft snapped in two. Only then, in the
middle of nowhere, did I realise that one spare paddle shared
between two canoeists wasn't enough. Surely so rare an event as
a paddle breaking isn't going to happen twice on one expedition,
I had been saying to myself for the past fifteen years. But here we
were with our journey hardly begun and no good answer as to
what we'd do if we had another similar mishap.

Once Michael and I were clear of Kerrera and into the Firth of
Lorn the wind was noticeably fresher and straight into our faces.
Well, maybe two and a half hours for the crossing. The sun broke
through. Grey skies re-formed into fairy castles, galleons in full
sail, towering snow-clad mountains. To our right Loch Linnhe
sparkled into the distance; to our left, some fifteen miles away,
the Garvellach Isles dented the horizon. A shaft of sunlight
picked out the white lighthouse off the end of Lismore. White
sails tilted in the breeze. All around us the peaks of Mull, Morven,
Appin and Lorn presented their purple profiles. Cloudscape,
seascape and landscape merged into one big bubble of pleasure
which swelled inside me and burst into a yell of pure joy.

Kayak bows bumped softly through fleets of translucent,
purple-veined jellyfish, spaceships hovering in a greenish void.
Lismore reminded me of the coracle race thirteen centuries ago
between St Moluag and St Columba. I told Michael the story as
we paddled along. But here is the old Hebridean account:

> St Moluag was sailing towards Lismore when he beheld a boat
> carrying St Columba for the Lismore shore at highest speed. St
> Columba's craft was the faster. When Moluag saw that he was
> likely to be beaten he seized an axe, cut off his little finger,
> threw it on the beach some distance away, and cried out, 'My
> flesh and blood have first possession of the island, and I bless
> it in the name of the Lord.'

We rested on our paddles, feeling the lure of Mull's south coast with its miles of sea cliffs and headlands receding westwards. Why not alter our plan? But the south coast was more exposed. Supposing there was a change of weather or wind direction? Long sections of that coast had no landing places, no escape. And there were only two of us. Three was a better number for a trip like that. Two canoeists could more easily rescue a comrade in the water than could a person on his own; and, in the event of an accident, the awful dilemma of whether to stay with the injured person or to go for help might be avoided. Besides, the thought of that broken shaft niggled at the back of my mind. What would we do if we were down to a single paddle between us? The distances were too great to make one of us towing the other a practical solution. All things considered, we decided to keep to our original plan and go for the Sound of Mull.

For the first three hours we had made visible progress. True, the wind had strengthened against us, but landmarks had continued to move in relation to each other, trees and houses on Mull had grown steadily bigger, the gap was obviously closing. And then, as if we had run into some invisible barrier, Duart Point refused to come any nearer. We were, by then, paddling almost parallel to the coast of Mull, but about half a mile off shore. The same wretched farmhouse, the same dreary telegraph pole, the same sneering mountain peak hovered endlessly opposite my left shoulder, mocking my frantic spurts to try and shift them behind me. Wind and tide could not account for this barrier, nor could the fact that we had been putting out energy since four o'clock that morning; it was a psychological rather than a physical barrier. Once we were more than two-thirds of the way across, we had begun to expect things to look closer, to anticipate the pleasures of stretching our legs; it was the old trap, the watched pot, the mind up to its tricks again. Do we never learn? So strongly did I crave proof that I was, in fact, moving forward that I turned off course and headed straight for the nearest land. Only when I was within spitting distance of the rocks did I resume my correct course. Oh, the relief of seeing my bows sliding past nearby things! The boost to my morale was such that in no time at all I was way ahead of Michael who had stayed further out. At last we reached Duart Point. It had taken us more than four hours. We had missed the ebb tide.

'For a moment there, you looked so desperate to reach this side, I thought you were going to cut off a finger and throw it ashore!' Michael said, when he caught up with me.

Rounding the point into the Sound of Mull we found that the wind was funnelling down it, even stronger than before. The sea was being whipped up, drenching us in spray. The sky was overcast again. The next half mile up the sound took us one and a half hours. We gave up and decided to make camp.

Paddling a fully loaded canoe through the water is one thing, carrying it, albeit only one end of it, is something else . . . particularly when the tide is out and the beach a hundred yards away. On the flat machair beyond the beach, we found a gorse bush, not a very big one, but big enough to give shelter from the wind. Michael erected the tent and got the stove going for a brew-up of tea, while I toured the beach for firewood. Rotting handfuls broken from a stranded tree trunk, the ribs from the skeleton of an old rowing boat, fish boxes, stray branches, sculptured pieces of driftwood, bleached and polished by the sea . . . the pile grew bigger. At last, the work done, we changed into dry clothes. On returning from our previous trip, Michael had expressed the opinion that the most dangerous thing about the whole expedition had been my cooking. So, while the master chef demonstrated his skills, I cheated on my fire lighting test by dousing my pile in some special fuel intended for barbecues. After a meal which must have considerably lightened the load in our canoes, we contemplated the sodden clothes we would have to put on again the next day. We always carried clothes-pegs and line, but the air was too damp and cold for our gear to have a chance of drying out. However, the same wind that had soaked us and chilled us now fanned our fire into a roaring, crackling fury. We stood in the dark, holding up our clothes, one by one, to the fire, watching the steam rise off them. To speed up the process I fixed my white underpants to the end of a branch and held them over the flames. Only for a few seconds did I lift my eyes to admire the stars through a break in the clouds, but it was long enough for streaks the colour of burnt toast to appear on my pants and for parts to sort of curl up and shrivel.

'That will impress the lads with the heat of your passion!' Michael said.

Sitting by the dying embers, I examined the broken paddle. Supposing we did need it? The first thing would be to dry out the broken ends over a fire and apply the superglue which was a part of our repair kit. If that didn't work the next best thing would be to try to hold the shaft together by means of splints, forced under the rubber drip-rings and tightly taped. Well, we'd find out soon enough what fortunes tomorrow brought.

Sunday morning was grey and spotting with rain. The wind was blowing from the north-west, as it had done yesterday, and was every bit as strong. Rather than battle against it, we decided to retrace our route down the Sound and head for the cliffs we had admired before. In their lee we should be sheltered from the worst of these blasts.

The rolling motion of the wind-driven waves pushing us along was so different from the bucking ride you get when bashing into them head on. Behind us a large MacBrayne's ferry pulled out of Craignure, bound for Oban: we altered course. Canoeists don't argue with vessels of that size, whatever the rule book might say. It, too, altered course, continuing to head straight for us. We altered course again. And still it aimed straight at us. 'Surely it'll see us and give us a wide berth,' I thought. It didn't. Huge metal bows sliced straight at us, producing a turn of speed unusual in me for that hour of the morning. The ferry swept past, churning up the waters which, seconds before, we had occupied. What with the extra adrenalin coursing through our bodies by courtesy of MacBrayne's Ltd, and the fact that the wind and the tide were both going our way, we covered the distance to Duart Point in one quarter the time it had previously taken us in the opposite direction.

The cliffs were astounding. For the next three hours we paddled along one of the most beautiful stretches of coastline I have ever encountered. More than any other part of the three-day trip this is the jewel I lift most often from the treasure chest; this is the experience which glows most warmly inside me; the memory I draw upon most frequently to put the petty events of life in their true perspective. Basalt geometry, hexagonal forms, giant blocks; sills like crazy, tilting staircases; deep, dark grooves and clefts splitting the rock for hundreds of feet; castles, buttresses, ramparts and fairy towers; hanging gardens of unexpectedly lush vegetation clinging to vertical faces; waterfalls, tumbling scree, gorges and narrow wooded valleys; wild goats bounding effortlessly in single file up rocky slopes; a hawk soaring and hovering on the updraft. And the sea. The sea pounding the base of the cliffs; the sea sluicing between galleries of smooth and blackly shining sculptures; the sea gurgling, sighing, moaning into dark caves and fissures, compressing the air till it exploded like cannon-shot.

Neither of us wanted it to end. We should have been tired, but so completely were we in the thrall of this coastline that no such idea visited us. We glided from ink-black waters into patches of emerald green, then blue-grey and green again, stopping opposite a canyon which cut through the rock for about twenty or thirty yards, ending in a small beach of shining wet pebbles. Waves surged up the canyon, their height and steepness exaggerated by the narrowness of the constricting walls.

'I could take a really good photograph of you in there, Michael. You need only go a little way up it.'

'I've got a much better idea,' Michael said.

'What?'

'You go, and I'll take the photograph.'

*   *   *

There wasn't enough elbow-room in the canyon for paddling, so I pushed myself forward with a hand on each wall, trying to banish images from my mind of being trapped upside-down in the confined space, all too aware of the next surge rushing upon me from behind. It hurled me forward like a dart. Only then did I see the large boulders just below the surface. Luck rather than skill guided my bows between them and dumped me on the smaller pebbles. In my haste I half fell out of the canoe, barking my shins on the boulders, dragging my craft up the little beach before the next surge could batter it to pieces. The beach was backed by steep cliffs. The only approach to it was from the sea, down the canyon that was too narrow for any vessel except a slim kayak. Was I the first person ever to stand here? I wondered. Then I discovered that, so tight was the space, I couldn't turn my kayak round. Nothing for it but to reverse out. I was hardly in the water before, with one big suck, the retreating undertow deposited me beside Michael.

'How about one more headland before we start looking for a campsite?' he said.

Between one tier of cliffs and another, on a flat, green shelf, wooded with oak and beech, we erected the tent. A waterfall tumbled from the landward cliffs into a rock pool. Below us, the sea kept up its onslaught, driving into crevices with such force that spouts twenty feet high rose into the air, falling just short of the tent. It was the perfect campsite. Not even the rain, which had now set into a light but steady drizzle, could spoil it for us. Our only hesitation in opting for this site had been the nature of the small cove in which we had landed. Entering it had been easy enough, but exiting from it tomorrow might present problems. When we arrived it was almost low tide. By tomorrow morning, however, the tide would be higher and the sea would be breaking over a belt of boulders halfway up the cove. We spent a long time, while that part of the beach was still visible, working out a route through the boulders, even moving one of them to give ourselves a clear exit.

Michael got the stove going for the soup. Between us we had one tin of vegetable soup and one of oxtail. Mull Broth, we named it. The pan was still generously endowed with this morning's porridge – all part of the famous recipe, we decided. Whilst gathering firewood under the trees I found a mushroom. Into the broth it went . . . as did a crumbling and sodden heap that had once been a packet of biscuits. The hoods of our anoraks were up for protection, not from the rain but from dark clouds of midges. We huddled over a sulky, smoky fire which did nothing to dry the clothes festooning the branches above, but at least kept the tormenting swarms at bay while we drank our broth.

'Special protein-enriched broth,' Michael said as he stirred in a score or more of midges who had volunteered themselves as an addition to the recipe.

I fell asleep that night to the sound of the rain drumming on the tent, the waterfall, the sea crashing and exploding below us, an owl hooting, and a herd of wild goats grumbling to themselves as they chewed seaweed in the cove.

Next morning, heart-rending cries filled the air. Michael was pulling on his wet clothes.

'You won't come to any harm through being wet, even for days on end, provided you keep warm,' I said severely.

The canoes were packed and ready to go. We were tempted to continue westwards, but in order to be back at our starting point on the mainland by four or five in the afternoon, now was when we should start retracing our route. As predicted, the sea was thundering over the boulders in the cove in a way that made our kayaks seem frail and vulnerable. We dithered, reminding ourselves more times than was necessary of the exact angle we needed for a clean exit. Michael waited for the incoming wave that adds the vital extra inch of depth, then, with a push from me directing him through the gap, he was committed . . . he was clear. My turn. Just as I launched, a freak wave broke right over my head. I paddled hard to get free of the churning waters and was soon beside Michael at the mouth of the cove.

'Never mind about being completely soaked through,' Michael said cheerfully. 'It won't do you any harm.'

The wind had shifted direction. Big waves were rolling east-wards parallel to our coast, catching us up, lifting us, throwing us forward, then dropping us in the trough behind them as they careered onwards. Michael's replies to my conversation seemed strangely vague. Of course! I should have realised straight away: this was the biggest sea that Michael had yet encountered and, until you get used to it, running with the waves is probably the most difficult motion of all to control. The waves grew steadily bigger, hissing up behind us at about head height. Suddenly the waves were very much bigger, steeper and more confused.

'I hope it doesn't get any worse than this!' Michael shouted above the noise of the breaking seas, an edge to his voice.

'It won't last!' I shouted back. 'Just a few minutes and we'll be through it.'

We were passing a headland. There must be a sill of rock jutting from it, making the sea shallower at this point so that, not only was the natural motion of the waves being broken up, but also each wave was steepening as its base was slowed down by friction with the bottom, allowing its own crest to catch up with it and climb more vertically above it. I maintained a position behind Michael where I could see him all the time, reflecting, as we plunged and tossed past the headland, on my original deci-sion that this was not a good stretch of coast for a two-man expe-dition. If he capsized, would I be able to rescue him single-handed in these conditions? Yes, I was fairly certain I could . . . none the less, I hoped I wasn't about to be called upon to prove it. Then we were through the bad bit. Michael was more relaxed. He'd had a brief taste of what it could be like and he'd discovered he could cope.

'Brief, that's the point,' Michael said. 'Long enough to sample it without it becoming an ordeal. And knowing it was going to end made all the difference. If you hadn't told me it wouldn't last long, I'm not sure how I'd have coped.'

We talked about the kind of mental as well as physical toughness needed to survive. The cliffs came to an end. We had passed along exactly the same stretch of beautiful coastline as yesterday and barely noticed it. Today the sea had held our attention completely and utterly. Lunch in a silver-sanded bay, then the crossing back to the mainland.

Once Gylen Castle on the end of Kerrera was behind us, we relaxed, thinking the journey to be virtually over. It wasn't. The last hour and a half was the hardest of the whole trip. The tide in full flow out of the Sound of Kerrera met the wind head on, producing rank upon rank of closely packed and very steep waves. Hardly had the canoe plunged into one deep trough before it was balancing on some steep pinnacle. In the midst of all this, Michael's red balaclava floated by, still on the surface, which was something of a minor miracle since by then, having raced ahead, he was some three hundred yards in front of me. At last we made harbour. I brandished the red balaclava. It had been a great trip, a mixed trip with a taste of everything, a broth of a trip.

Chapter 17

Blazing Socks

Around Raasay

Instead of starting the four-hour drive to Kyle of Lochalsh at midday on the Friday, we didn't get going until after five o'clock; that is to say the battery of Michael's car didn't get going till then. On the way we talked about Brian Wilson and his book *Blazing Paddles* which describes his hair-raising solo journey by kayak right round the coast of Scotland. We wondered what sort of mileages per day we could build up to if we paddled regularly day after day for two months or more. We were not as fit as we'd been for our trip to the south coast of Mull this time a year ago. For a multitude of reasons we'd only done about half our usual mileage that season. Unfortunately, because of our late start, our planned circumnavigation of Raasay would have to be done in two, not two and a half days. At Kyle of Lochalsh a long queue of cars was being herded onto the ferry for Skye as we loaded our kayaks at a small adjacent slipway, struggling to defy Murphy's Law, Clause One of which states: 'Equipment needed always exceeds space available, however short the trip.' It was nine thirty in the evening. We hurried to make the most of the remaining light. Even twenty minutes of paddling before we unloaded everything again and made camp would be worth it. We would be off the mainland, out of sight of cars and roads and houses, able to believe that the expedition had begun. Next morning we were afloat by nine. A low mist hung over everything as we slammed through a choppy sea the colour of steel. Dampness invaded everything, but, oh, the relief of being free of the midges! We had nearly suffocated during the night rather than leave open the smallest crack in the tent through which the bloodthirsty hordes might pour; at breakfast we had stumbled about, unable to see properly with hats pulled down to the nose and hoods laced up to the eyebrows. Grey shapes, slightly greyer than the mist, occasionally showed themselves.

'Where are we heading?' Michael asked.

'I don't know. We're not on my map yet,' I said.

Murphy's Law, Clause Two, states that, no matter where you're going, you're always on the join between two maps, or on the line where it folds. We paddled north-westwards in the hope that the dance of the seven veils would eventually let slip a revealing glimpse. It did and we altered course, heading for Longay.

Longay, east side — diagonally slanting strata, pink cliffs, jagged spires which turned into cormorants, bays of deep bottle-green beneath overhangs. Rounding the north end of Longay we surprised a dozen or so seals lying on the rocks — brown, grey, white, all sizes. They flopped towards the edge and plunged into the sea, but two of them were slow off the mark. I raced up to them and raised my camera . . . only to find that I had come to the end of the reel. We stopped briefly for a brew-up of tea. Raasay was now visible, its east coast combining with Rona to form a seemingly continuous line of deepening purple stretching into the distance for twenty miles. Which way round should we do the circuit? We calculated that the flood tide at the Narrows of Raasay, the gateway to the island's west side, would be at its strongest and in opposition to us by the time we reached it. So we decided to avoid it and go up the east coast of Raasay.

An hour and a half and seven miles of lively, running sea later, we glided into a bay of clear, clear, liquid emerald. Fathoms down, shoals of brown fish swam above clean white sand. From one headland of the bay a waterfall tumbled into the sea. The sun came out. While I meditated, Michael collected fish-boxes and lit a fire. Our clothes were sodden, partly from spray, partly from perspiration. We stripped off and hung them out to dry. My white towelling socks I placed upwind of the fire, but near enough to feel the heat. I closed my eyes, enjoying the sun on my skin. When I opened my eyes, the wind had shifted and my socks resembled charred kippers.

'Oh no! Not again!'

'You should call your canoeing book 'Blazing Socks',' Michael chortled.

'I bet Murphy's got something to do with this!' I muttered darkly.

The next ten miles rivalled the south coast of Mull for sheer beauty. I have never before seen cliffs of such profusion of form: mini-Dolomites, fairy tale castles, the fortress walls of Zimbabwe: and jumbled cubes of striped rock, eroded and pitted along the grain, which brought images tumbling into my mind – honeycombs, herring-bone tweed, Liquorice allsorts, Henry Moore, dice, cross-hatching. I had been telling Michael about an idea I'd had to create miniature ceramic landscapes, but nothing I could have made up would have equalled this coastline for inventiveness. Further inland, occasionally emerging from the cloud, was the strangely truncated top of Dun Caan, jutting upwards like the spine of Tyrranosaurus Rex. Not far from the south side of Dun Caan are deep pits caused by earth movements. In cold weather water vapour rising from them condenses, giving the peak the appearance of a smoking volcano. Everything was so green. Bright green slopes sweeping up to the base of the cliffs; and wooded precipices, not the occasional stunted tree growing out of the rock, but acres of vertical forest. Accompanying the unfolding of the drama, mile by mile, was the music of the sea whose deep base undertone boomed from dark vents along the waterline.

Afternoon was edging into evening. To maintain our schedule we must round the north end of Raasay before making camp for the night. Perhaps the next headland would be the final one . . . or the next . . . or maybe the one after that. At last the gap between Raasay and Rona appeared. We put into a little bay for another brew-up. A body working hard hour after hour while covered in waterproof garments sweats profusely and needs a large liquid intake. Turning the corner had boosted our morale. One more stint of paddling didn't seem quite such a bad idea.

'We'll keep going till seven-thirty, then stop at the first good campsite we see,' we agreed.

On emerging from the far end of the strait the horizon opened out. Spreading northwards into the dove-grey distance was the Minch; the headlands of the Trotternish Peninsula reached for the north-west and grabbed the horizon; and southwards the Sound of Raasay was a glinting aisle leading to the altar of the Cuillins draped in white. The whole motion of the sea changed. A gentle, undulating swell surged southwards from the Minch, revealing its hidden power only when it exploded on the shore. We could hear it from at least half a mile away. Ahead was a small island, Griana-Sgeir.

'That's the place for us!' Michael declared. 'The perfect campsite.'

He was right. Lush, ungrazed vegetation, giant daisies, enough driftwood to last the night, enough breeze to keep the midges away, a self-contained world we could encompass in five minutes, loaned to us temporarily by the seals and Arctic terns.

We were up at five next morning and on the water by seven. During the night there had been a downpour so heavy that, according to Michael, it had drowned even the sound of my snoring. Everything we possessed seemed to be on a scale that ranged from wet to absolutely sodden. But a bowl of hot porridge works wonders and the body soon warms to the paddling. Murphy's Law had been exerting its influence again – Clause Three: 'No matter how much you eat, what comes out of a packed canoe never fits back in again.' A dolphin broke the surface and my brooding thoughts, the peaks of Skye stuck their heads above the clouds, the strange obelisk known as the Old Man of Storr emerged from the mist and the west coast of Raasay suddenly changed into a series of intriguing sea-caves and cliff-girt coves pierced by wild gorges. 'Just the place for smugglers,' I thought. Later, I read that Raasay and Rona had, in fact, been the haunt of outlaws and smugglers. An early account describes the fleet of 'thieves, ruggairs and reivairs' that operated from Acarsaid Mor, on the west side of Rona. We stopped in one of the coves to replenish our supply of fresh water, reaching it by passing under a natural arch. A rushing burn had carved a course across the pebbled beach into a high domed cave at the opposite end of which were framed views of the hills behind Portree on Skye. Minutes later we paddled into a cave; it grew darker, narrower, the echoing cries of the cormorants and the gurgling groans of the water became louder, then we turned a corner and found ourselves paddling out of another cave some thirty yards further along the coast.

We took 'lunch' at ten-thirty in the morning. It rained. Not even my special lifeboat matches would light the stove. The warmest place, we decided, was in the kayaks. As we rounded a headland just before the narrows a force six or seven wind sprang upon us, taking us completely by surprise. We battled to make headway, until, at last, we could turn left through the narrows and set out across Kyle Mor (or Caol Mor) for Scalpay. Now our left arms were doing twice as much work as our right as the wind constantly caught at our sterns, pushing the bows upwind. From a point somewhere near the middle of this kyle I enjoyed what must be one of the finest views in the west of Scotland. Here was a kind of crossroads of magnificent panoramas – north: the vista up the Sound of Raasay; west: looking up Loch Sligachan into the heart of the Cuillins; south: down the Kyle of Scalpay to the Red Hills in the south of Skye; east: the mainland, Loch Kishorn, Loch Carron, and the mountains of Applecross. I would have enjoyed it all the more if my left arm hadn't ached so much.

Scalpay. Seals singing on the rocks. Another brew-up. Beginning to feel tired. Such an abundance and variety of cloud: wispy, feathery cirrus, cumulus billowing upwards shining in the sun, dark stratus, all in the same sky. Then the crossing to Pabay in a frisky sea of spanking blue, sparkling with white tops, so exhilarating that I forgot I was tired. One final leg to go. With the white lighthouse at the Kyle of Lochalsh catching the sun and guiding us home, we paddled on, surrounded by the dark purple silhouettes of the hills. Slowly, very slowly, the lighthouse grew taller. At last we were passing it and entering Loch Alsh. To our right the bright little houses of Kyleakin greeted us like rows of children in party dresses. It was six-thirty in the evening. With only a few short breaks, we had been paddling for more than eleven hours since breaking camp on Griana-Sgeir. All things considered, the three of us had had a good trip, Michael and Murphy and me.

Chapter 18

Gale Force from the Garvellachs

A stormy return from the Garvellach Isles

All night our tents had heaved and panted, their edges cracking like machine-gun fire. And now, in the morning, the sea was white-flecked with southward speeding waves. We were on Garbh Eileach, the largest island in the Garvellach chain. Easdale, our destination on the mainland, lay seven miles to the north-east. Should we attempt the crossing or not? Lofty, the leader of our six-person expedition, was undecided.

'The shipping forecast is force seven, gusting to eight,' he said.

We didn't need to be told that anything above eight was a gale-force wind.

'We've both got to be back at work tomorrow,' Ken and Joe reminded him.

We sized up the situation. Over confidence and male pride figured large in our reckoning. The previous day the six of us had paddled our kayaks eighteen miles from Mull to Garbh Eileach through mountainous swell and winds of force six or seven. We had coped with it well. We were the best, we told ourselves. We were the greatest. Besides, none of us was going to be the first to back down – not with Heather in the group. The fact that she was probably the best woman sea-canoeist in Britain weighed less with us than the fact that she was female and only nineteen. Then there were members of the British Girls' Exploration Society (Senior Branch) who were occupying a bothy on the island.

'I don't think you should go,' one of them said.

That decided it.

Half an hour out from the Garvellachs I knew we had made a serious mistake. This was no force seven gusting to eight. We were paddling straight into a full force nine gale. Tons of solid grey sea, curling at the top, swept towards me. Up rose my kayak, up to where the shrieking wind would have torn the paddle from my grasp had I not clung to it with all my strength, up to where the spume was driven blindingly into my face. Then, the downward plunge and the next wave looming over me, blotting out the 300-foot-high hills of the Garvellachs.

There could be no question of turning back. Running with the waves, particularly when they roll up behind you and overtake you, is far more difficult than heading into them. We were committed to our decision.

In calm weather, the seven-mile crossing would have taken about an hour and a half. That day, in the first hour of hard paddling, I moved forward twenty yards. The group was scattered over an area of about a square mile. Occasionally, someone would rise into sight only to disappear again, leaving me alone on the empty, tossing expanse.

Another advancing wall of water; and another; never-ending ranks of waves, each one threatening to break over me, drenching me, disorientating me, hurling me sideways. Down into a deep grey gulf, bracing myself for the next oncoming crest.

After the second hour of paddling, the same white house on the shore was still opposite my starboard bow. This couldn't be happening to me. It couldn't. Keep going, keep going! To rest for even a minute would be to lose every hard-earned inch. The sea slapped my face. The dream-bubble burst as the painful, sharp-edged truth of my predicament pierced my mind and twisted inside my gut. If I made a mistake and capsized, death was only minutes away. There was no possibility of rolling my kayak up again in these conditions. If I paddled until exhaustion claimed me, my life expectancy was a few hours at the most. No profound thoughts about death visited me, only a dull ache of regret. Above everything else, I was possessed by a fierce, animal instinct for survival and an acute desire to avert the actual moment of dying, the agony of drawing the cold ocean into my lungs.

The enemy was not the sea. The enemy was fear, cold, fatigue and loneliness. And the greatest of these is loneliness. If I saw one of my companions capsize I was going to leave him to his fate. Our rescue drills would be useless in seas as steep as this. Each of the others would have made the same decision. I could expect no help. Yet my heart lifted whenever I saw I was not alone in this inhospitable place and that another human being shared my travail. Every muscle in my body whimpered, 'I'm tired, I'm so tired. I can't go on!' But when your life depends on it you do go on.

In those third and fourth hours, I entered uncharted mental states, plunging from crests of pure joy into troughs of terror and despair. Screaming with rage at my kayak I hammered it with my fists and hurled vile abuse at it for not keeping a straight course, threatening to chop it into little pieces and burn it. And the next instant I was singing at the top of my voice with sheer exhilaration at the power, the splendour, the magnificence of this mighty ocean. Surely this was the closest Man could ever come to the elemental forces. And then, for a thousand different reasons, the salt of my tears mingled with that of the sea.

South side of Garbh Eileach, Garvellach Isles

Some of this emotional see-sawing was caused, I knew, by the onset of hypothermia. Recognising and understanding the symptoms helped me to hold it at bay. But my stamina was ebbing away. My hands had lost all feeling, cramp was beginning to grip my forearms and stomach. My co-ordination was falling apart. I tried to paddle and completely missed the water. I can't go on! This time, I really can't! I stared stupidly at the wooden implement in my hands. What was it? Oh, yes, a paddle. But what you did with it I could not think. An extra large chunk of water struck me beam on and sent me skidding down its steep reverse side. Instinctively I reacted, made the correct stroke and was paddling again with energy drawn from some secret well deep inside me.

Hugh's yellow kayak appeared on my right. 'How are you doing?' I shouted.

'Bloody glad to see you!'

His face was ashen, tense, etched with fatigue. Hugh's need of me kept me going. As long as he could see me paddling beside him he wouldn't give up. Suddenly Heather was there too, on an adjacent wave.

'The tide's turning!' she yelled above the din. 'If you can hold your own, the tide will carry you home! Just one more hour!' Heather's message of hope, the white house at last beginning to shift, encouraging Hugh: these things brought me into Easdale harbour.

I made landfall. Ken sat on the beach, his head in his hands. Joe lay face down, groaning. Heather nodded to me and smiled. I was too numb, both physically and mentally, to respond. I discovered later she had found each one of us in that storm and given us hope. Lofty, who was already in the car park above the harbour, opened his car door. The wind wrenched it off its hinges and sent it scudding across the tarmac like a leaf until it crumpled against a wall. Nobody said anything. The only sounds were the wind, the sea and someone close by quietly sobbing.

All six of us had survived five hours in a force nine gale, but none of us would ever again claim to be the greatest. That title we reserve for the sea.

Chapter 19

A Chorus of Islands

Orkney

Twenty-six years have gone by since being caught in that storm on the way back from the Garvellachs. Michael is still paddling with me, Archie is back in the fold, and Ian and Colin have joined the little group of like-minded paddlers. Our hair is now greyer or, in the case of Archie and myself, conspicuous by its absence. In the intervening years I have retired from my job, published several more books, had a coronary by-pass operation and a new metal knee joint, and kept paddling through thick and thin. Michael, instead of being the wide-eyed novice of yesteryear, is now the assured and intrepid leader of our group. I am content to relax and enjoy the scenery rather than having to keep at least one eye on the others. It's somebody else's turn do the calculating and the worrying. We are all using more modern kayaks than in the previous episodes described, except for Archie. One thing that hasn't changed – the one constant factor – is Archie's kayak, 'Spirit of Budge Budge', made by himself to his own design. Like an otter marking its territory, it continues to leave orange paint on the rocks up and down the length of the Scottish coast. In July 2002, the comparatively recent past, Michael, Ian, Colin and I rented a house at Harray on Mainland Orkney as our kayaking base (Archie couldn't make it for this particular trip). Our reasoning was that it was going to be a tough week of paddling and that we could not sustain the level of performance needed unless we were eating and sleeping well and able to dry our clothes at the end of each day. Kayak-camping for a whole week had lost its appeal. Perhaps we were all getting older and liking our creature comforts more. Not that we were admitting to this. Our other strategy for extracting the best out of the week was to make contact with John Mowatt, an experienced Orkney paddler. He accompanied us on several outings and, thanks to his advice, we did not have to find out the hard way which were the worthwhile routes to do and which were not. Strong tides race in and out of this archipelago, which totals something over 70 islands, varying considerably in their behaviour and timing from one place to another. The Clyde Cruising Club's sailing directions for this area begin with a dire warning, and mentions of overfalls, violent races, eddies, roosts and seven-knot tides pop up on almost every other page. A certain Murdoch Mackenzie, writing in 1745, had this to say about tides in general and the Orkney tides in particular:

> All the philosophers since Newton's time have considered only, or principally, the influence of the Moon in elevating and depressing the tides. Their several directions, velocities and other affections resulting from the influence of the land, shoals and wind remain still as inexplicable and as little known as ever.

As far as I'm concerned not much has changed in the two and a half centuries or so since that was written, and John's local knowledge about these matters was invaluable. Our decision was reinforced by the CCC sailing directions which advise that, 'in such a complex cruising ground, local knowledge takes on a special significance.'

Morning found us driving towards the Bay of Skaill. There's something about the Orkneys that's like being on the sea – the gently undulating countryside, the big open skies. Compared to the Hebrides or Shetland, the Orkneys are lush and fertile. As the old saying goes: 'An Orcadian is a farmer with a boat, while a

Shetlander is a fisherman with a croft.' As our car topped one of the rolling hills we could see islands spread out like shards of broken pottery, island upon island. The sense that there is always something more, something beyond the next island, or round the next headland, is one of the lures of Orkney. Fourteen of the islands are inhabited, but exactly how many islands there are depends on one's definition of an island. To an Orcadian, it is a piece of land on which you can keep a sheep for a year. Smaller than that and it's called a rock.

Launching at Bay of Skaill, we headed south along the magnificent Old Red Sandstone cliffs of Yesnaby – miles of jutting headlands, like the prows of a battle fleet heading out to sea. The cliffs fall sheer into the water, allowing us to paddle close to them, marvelling at their scale and steepness. Even on this calm day, there was sufficient turbulence off the steep walls to demand our attention, so that we paid scant heed to the grandeur of it all. In the more accessible bays these cliffs draw rock climbers from far and wide. The names of the routes give some idea of their hazardous nature: Skull Splitter, Thrutch, Sink or Swim, Nemesis.

The sea swilled idly around the big arched stack known as Yesnaby Castle while we sunbathed in the nearby bay. I have been shown photographs, though, of this tall stack all but submerged in a winter storm. We could see for ourselves the way the turf along the cliff tops, 300 feet above sea level, had been eroded by high flung seas. John spoke of spray being blown six miles inland.

While we ate our sandwiches, Ian and I told John about the Western Isles Challenge which we had taken part in several years previously. It was a relay race for teams of four or five people along the length of the Hebrides from Barra in the south to the Butt of Lewis in the north. Provided you passed through all the check points and did a specified proportion of the race on foot, you could cover the remaining distance in a number of ways – on a bicycle, swimming, by kayak. Part of the fascination of the race lay in working out the best strategy, whether it was quicker to swim 200 metres across a loch or cycle 20 miles round it, whether

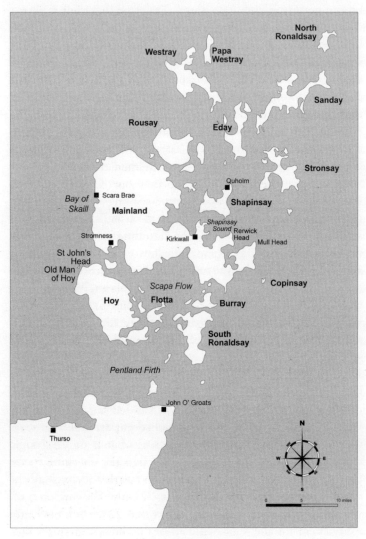

The Orkney Islands

running over a couple of peaks was quicker than kayaking round the coast. The formula was different for each team, of course, depending on its strengths and weaknesses. It didn't take me long to realise that picking a good support team was as important as picking the actual racers. Several teams came to grief because their back-up wasn't working properly. Thus, runner A would arrive at point X ready to jump onto a bicycle only to find that the said vehicle was still at point W where it had last been used; or runner B would be waiting for a car to take him to point Z where he would do his next section of running, only to find that no car came for him because it was still delivering a kayak to point Y where it would be needed when runner C arrived there to hand over the baton. Luckily, our team included a married couple who were both computer wizards. They produced a complete schedule of exactly what everyone should be doing and where they should be doing it at any specific moment of the day. The computer print-out of the master plan was about thirty feet long. The wife in this partnership, who was German, oversaw the enforcement of the plan with admirable Teutonic efficiency. Ian was the star of the team, being the only one who did a bit of everything – some fell-running, some cycling, some kayaking, and the compulsory orienteering section. I only did the main kayaking bits. I found I did best on the days when the sea was rough, which was when my experience gave me an advantage over the others, all of whom were a lot younger than me. The race, which lasted five days, started with 52 teams. Every day, teams dropped out through injury, or because they found the going too tough, but mainly through being disqualified by not passing through the checkpoints or failing to complete the allotted section for the day within the cut-off time. By the fifth day there were only 30 teams left, of which ours was one. Our final position was 22nd. Not brilliant, but not bad for the team with by far the highest average age. When I entered our team for the Veteran section, I had thought that a veteran must mean people in their fifties. Actually, it meant that the average age of the team should not be less than 35! I was still looking for the fifth member of our team when this fact finally reached my brain. I could have selected someone who was minus ten years old and our team would still have qualified as Veterans.

Another day saw us paddling out from Stromness, aiming for the north end of the island of Hoy, with the intention of going down its western side.

'Have you got sixpence for Bessie Millie?' John called to me.

Seeing my blank look, he explained that Bessie Millie was the spaewife or witch who sold favourable winds to sea captains for sixpence. She is supposed to have been visited by Sir Walter Scott in 1814, when she was over 90. She told him the story of John Gow the pirate, upon which Scott based his novel, *The Pirate*.

St John's Head, at the north-west end of Hoy, was a stunning, neck-craning experience. At 1,134 feet, it is the highest vertical sea cliff in the British Isles. As I looked up at its dizzying, cloud-framed rim, it seemed to tilt, toppling me sideways. I discovered to my cost that another hazard in staring upwards was being shat upon, sicked upon or otherwise bombarded by the huge numbers of shags, fulmars, kittiwakes, puffins and rock doves which resided on the cliffs and used the multiple ledges as high diving boards. Not far inland from where we were, John told us, is Britain's most northerly woodland.

All the time, standing proudly ahead of us was the Old Man of Hoy in hues of pink and red, the tallest sea stack in Britain, 450 feet high, rising from its plinth of igneous rock that connects it to the mainland. From a distance it has a tottering, slightly unbalanced appearance, like a tower of wooden bricks built by a three-year-old. Although any Orkney fisherman would have said this was a calm day, landing at its base was tricky. There was only one narrow gut between the rocks where it was feasible, up which funnelled every wave in sight. Colin was detailed to go first and be the one to assist the rest of us as we quickly scrambled out. He had a plastic boat, you see, which wouldn't be damaged so easily.

His plastic boat was an excuse, I mean a reason, that served the rest of us very well on several occasions.

The Old Man of Hoy is even more of an attraction for climbers than the Yesnaby cliffs. The first ascent was made over a period of three days by Tom Patey, Rusty Baillie and Chris Bonnington in 1966. At the time, it was a superbly daring ascent. Now between 20 and 50 ascents of the Old Man are made per year and seven different routes have been pioneered on it, of which the original is the easiest. None of the routes looked even remotely easy to us as we stood at its base gazing up in awe.

There is no mention of this striking feature in the old Orkney sagas. And on seventeenth and eighteenth century maps the Old Man is not shown and therefore presumably not yet formed since a headland is marked at this point. However, by 1819, when the landscape painter William Daniell visited Hoy and sketched the site, the headland had been eroded into a stack and arch with the twin legs that gave the Old Man its name. Soon after this a severe storm washed away one of the legs, leaving the stack more or less as we see it now. The future will almost certainly bring the total demise of the Old Man. There is already a large 40-metre crack running vertically from the top of the stack which threatens its upper reaches. And waves will continue to erode its base until the entire pillar collapses.

Returning the way we had come, I reflected sadly that these beautiful cliffs used to be shelled by the Royal Navy for target practice. Towards the end of the day there was an exhilarating run through a long tunnel which pierced the headland. The swell had got up a bit and was sweeping through it. The quiet spells between one swell and the next lasted just long enough to lure us into attempting the traverse.

We went one by one, each waiting for the right moment. When it was my turn, I could hear the swell enter the tunnel behind me, roaring like an express train. I paddled like crazy, shooting out at the other end amidst a welter of foam, adrenalin pumping, yelling like a madman.

The next day we launched at Kirkwall on the other side of Orkney Mainland. The strong tidal stream in Shapinsay Sound was an experience not to be missed, so John informed us. It was almost flat calm. Apart from rippling patches, small whirlpools and overfalls, all was peaceful. I appeared not to be moving at all, although the current was running at a good six knots. The shores of Shapinsay, on the other hand, were racing past at an incredible speed. Try as I might, I could not convince myself that it was me who was moving and not the island. We ferry glided across to Shapinsay, just catching it by the tail before it whizzed by, and landed for a brew-up.

'What's ferry gliding?' a friend asked me when he read the draft version of this account. I could tell he was thinking Dunoon car ferry with wings. I explained that it is a technique for crossing a strong current. If, for example, the current is rushing at you from your left, you exert a counter force by paddling on the right-hand side of your kayak only. The effect is rather like squeezing a pip. The two opposite forces make the kayak shoot forward in a straight line across the current.

John informed us that Quholm in the north-east of Shapinsay was the birthplace of the father of the American writer Washington Irving, author of *Rip van Winkle*. Some Orcadians claim a link between the Rip van Winkle story and the local folklore of creatures called trowes, a type of troll. Colin opened a can of beer. This reminded me that Shapinsay, like Birsay and several other Orkney islands, used to be a major exporter of kelp and kelp products in the nineteenth century. Apart from having thick kelp forests in their inshore zones, they had the advantage that the severe winter storms uprooted the kelp and washed it onto the beach, harvesting it for the islanders. Kelp or 'tangle' was originally burned for its high potash and soda content for use in glass and soap manufacture. With the discovery of other sources of these chemicals, kelp harvesting declined, but revived again as a source of iodine. This in turn declined in the 1930s when iodine could be extracted more cheaply from Chilean nitrates. However, in recent years tangle has been collected again for the extraction of alginates, whose gelling and emulsifying properties are used in products as diverse as tomato ketchup, postage stamps, medical dressings and beer (added to aid head retention). When I told Colin about the head on his beer, he said that, as a diver, he had always been wary of going into the dense kelp forests in case of meeting a giant eel lurking there.

The conversation turned to all the places we had yet to go in our kayaks. There was so much still waiting for us to discover. In that wonderfully informative book *Scottish Islands* the author, Hamish Haswell-Smith, states that Scotland has 165 saltwater islands larger than one hundred acres. To land on every single one of those in a kayak . . . now there's a project to think about!

Many lasting memories of kayak trips, we agreed, were associated not just with the kayaking, but with the journey through wild and beautiful places, with things we did on the rest days or when the weather prohibited paddling. There was the ascent of Stac Polly with the Summer Isles laid out on a silver sea below us. And there was the time when we had a punctured tyre. Somehow, with five eager helpers all milling about, the same wheel that was removed was put back on again! But I won't mention the shaming episode of the taxi – the time when, returning up Loch Sunnart, we were making such little progress against an incredibly strong wind that we stopped and phoned for a taxi. No, I definitely won't mention that.

Boarding the express train again, we let ourselves be carried eastwards past Rerwick Head and then on to Mull Head. The swell meeting the tidal stream was only a gentle one. Nevertheless, the sea became quite lumpy. Undoubtedly, with stronger winds and bigger swells the seas out here would be truly horrendous. All the time we were in the Orkneys we had this uneasy feeling that the weather, the tides, the islands themselves were playing a game of cat and mouse with us and could pounce at any moment; that at any hour, the brooding truce between the North Sea and the Atlantic would be broken and all hell would let loose.

Somewhere, in this menacing stretch, Colin and Michael saw what they described as 'a very big fish' breaking the surface. What it was they weren't sure, but the speed with which its tall fin cut through the water made Colin remark that he thought it might be a very large and excited shark and he hoped it wouldn't get too curious about us.

Turning south at Mull Head, we spent the rest of the day exploring this spectacular stretch of coastline. This was my first experience of such a wealth of caves, geos (Old Norse for a creek), chasms, canyons, arches and tunnels. No sooner had I been amazed and thrilled by one cave than the next was opening its mouth to receive me.

On entering some of them there was a strong and unnerving sensation of going downhill. It took me a while to realise that this illusion was created by the gently sloping strata on either side.

It was the kind of day when you don't cover many miles, but you work hard all the same – perhaps harder than a steady paddle – turning, stopping, starting, reversing, manoeuvring in and out of narrow places. One of the things that impressed me most was the absolute darkness of the caves. Once you turned a corner, out of sight of the cave mouth, the blackness was a tangible, unnerving presence. I used this experience in my novel, *Red Fox Running* (a novel for teenagers set in Greenland), when Adam and his Inuit girlfriend, Pipaluk, kayak into a cave:

They bumped and scraped round a corner into complete darkness.

Adam had never met total and absolute darkness before. He could not see his own hand in front of his face. 'Pipaluk, are you there?'

'Yes.' He guessed from the echoes that this was a smaller, narrower chamber.

Being cut off from the force of the swell, it was calmer. Afraid of bumping his head, Adam inched cautiously into the blackness. He kept one wall within touching distance of his paddle. Their hissing breath, the loud dripping, the water sobbing in cracks and fissures filled the darkness with eerie noises.

Adam felt the reassuring bump of Pipaluk's bows against his stern.

'I'm glad you're with me, Pipaluk.'

'Same here.'

I, too, was glad, in those caves in Orkney, not to be alone.

Five years later, in the summer of 2007, I found myself walking along the clifftops of the Deerness Peninsula towards Mull Head. Orkney was in our blood and it was inevitable that we would return. However, an embarrassingly stupid capsize a couple of weeks earlier had resulted in a shoulder injury which prevented me paddling with the others. While they – the usual culprits plus Archie – spent a week playing hide and seek with strong winds and dodging between the islands, I wandered afoot with my camera. Looking from the landward side through the narrow Gloup with its high, sheer rock walls I marvelled that we had dared enter it. Although it is true that kayakers see a hidden coastline, accessible only to a narrow craft with a shallow draft, it is equally true that tide tables and weather forecasts often dominate one's schedule, leaving little room for discovering other aspects of the area. So, it was as a walker and photographer that I saw Orkney with new eyes. For me, the most memorable day was when I took the 15-minute flight in an eight-seater plane from Kirkwall to North Ronaldsay, the most northerly isle in Orkney. I set out to walk round the island, but one hour later had progressed no more than 200 yards. There was so much to look at and photograph – old zig-zag dry stone walls etched with lichens, fields of oats rippling in the wind, flowered meadows like mediaeval tapestries, the wide open sky and seals basking on the off-shore rocks. A 13-mile stone wall runs round the island. Its purpose is not too keep the sheep in, but to confine them to the narrow stretch of beach between the wall and the sea where they live on seaweed. Domesticated ruminants, like cows and sheep, graze by day, then regurgitate the semi-digested cud and chew this by night to complete the digestive process. The North Ronaldsay sheep, however, have evolved in a different way. Their digestive cycle is determined by the tides so that they graze on the seaweed when it is exposed at low tide, then regurgitate and chew the cud when the seaweed is covered at high tide.

Back in 2002, we took a rest day in which I visited Skara Brae. This prehistoric village, dating from around 3000 BC, only came to light when it was exposed by a storm in 1824. It appealed to me that it was buried in a sandstorm in about 2450 BC and then uncovered by another storm 5,000 years later. A visitor to these islands once remarked, 'Whenever you go to Orkney it is as if a secret is being revealed'. I sensed something of that here, as I had in the dark, whispering caves.

Of greater interest to me, however, was the museum in Stromness. Here were things I could relate to more easily. There were many artefacts connected to Arctic whaling. The whaling fleets used to stop at Kirkwall to pick up Orkney men who were regarded as some of the hardiest and most reliable seamen. And there was a whole section about the Scottish Arctic explorer John Rae, born in Orkney in 1813. Rae was the first person to find any real clues as to what had happened to the ill-fated Franklin expedition, but in so doing he incurred the displeasure of the Victorian establishment by hinting that cannibalism might have occurred, and thus he never gained the recognition in his lifetime that he deserved.

The museum is also very informative about Scapa Flow which was Britain's chief naval base in both World Wars. It was here on 21 June 1919, the day the Armistice came to an end, that the surrendered German High Seas Fleet was scuttled on the command of its admiral. Fifty-two ships went to the bottom (5 battleships, 10 battle cruisers, 5 light cruisers, 32 destroyers). The salvage operations started in the early 1920s with most of the ships having been raised by the late 1930s. Fragments of ships are still being raised and, since Hiroshima, they have become an important source of quality radioactive free metals necessary for certain types of sensitive scientific instruments.

It was in Scapa Flow, too, that the *Royal Oak*, a Revenge-class battleship was sunk at anchor in October 1939. During both World Wars, German U-boats tried to attack British ships in Scapa Flow. The World War I attempts failed and the U-boats sunk. But, early in World War II, a U-boat penetrated Scapa Flow's defences and torpedoed the *Royal Oak* which quickly sank. Of the 1,400 crew, 833 were lost. The wreck is now a protected war grave. After the attack Winston Churchill ordered the construction of a series of causeways to block the eastern approaches to Scapa Flow. These were built by Italian prisoners of war who were being held in Orkney.

Our final trip was out to Copensay, east of Mainland. My most vivid memory of the trip is running ahead of a following sea (well, an overtaking sea, actually) toward the island's north-west point and then turning a sharp corner to find the island completely changed in character. Instead of angling up towards the top of a hill, crowned by a lighthouse, it abruptly transformed into a straight, vertical line of cliffs, teeming with seabirds – almost a mile of cliff packed with nesting fulmars, guillemots, razor bills and kittiwakes. The clamour of the birds, the wind whistling round the corner, the waves seething at the base of the cliff, this was the song of Orkney in full voice, in the language of sea and salt, filling my ears, filling the whole of me, like a wild and joyful chorus from the untamed elements of this planet.

Chapter 20

Speed, Bonnie Boat

Skye

I first knew Skye as a climber and hill walker and only later as a kayaker. In those earlier days the Cuillin Hills were my magnet. On 'The Isle of Mists' you are not often granted a clear view of the peaks, but when you are the bare ridges, spires, crags, gullies and long scree slopes are a magnificent sight. Most mountains are huge, bent and fractured strata of rock, but the Cuillins give the impression of being one enormous, solid, sculptured stone, or perhaps the protruding skeleton of the earth, scraped to the bone. One of the most memorable things about the Cuillins, for those who set foot on them, is the coarse, crystalline gabbro rock which provides so much friction that you can saunter, hands in pockets, up steep-angled slabs which would be almost impossible to climb anywhere else in Britain. Even with sheets of water sliding down them, you can walk over acres of pitted, riveted, abrasive slabs with no fear of a slip. And it was as a mountaineer that I first appreciated the description of Skye as 'the most beautiful witch of the western seas'. Beautiful undoubtedly; and witch-like too with its talons piercing the sky, and wild weather brewed up in high rock cauldrons – a place to cast a spell on you. We – Michael, Ian, Colin and I – launched our kayaks at Elgol in the southwest corner of Skye and headed into a strong wind across a choppy, slate-coloured Loch Scavaig towards Loch na Cuilce. In the far corner of the latter is a lonely little bay with a small landing place on sloping slabs. From there it is only a short walk into

Loch Coruisk in the heart of the Cuillins. Approaching it on foot is a long walk around the coast from either direction, or a hard day's scrambling if you come at it over the mountains. By water, in a small boat or kayak, is the easiest way to get there. Well, that's the theory anyway, but plugging straight into the wind, I began to have my doubts. It was the sort of wind where you can't stop for a rest for fear of being blown backwards and losing all the hard-won forward yards. I developed a steady rhythm, punching out the words and the tune of the 'Skye Boat Song':

> 'Speed bonnie boat like a bird on the wing
> Over the sea to Skye.'

Ahead lay the Black Cuillins, half shrouded in mist, dark, austere and stern, and yet, at the same time, alluring like a dusky maiden doing the Dance of the Seven Veils, revealing tantalising glimpses through vapoury layers. Behind and to my left were Rùm, Eigg, Muck and Canna. There was that time we had the idea of 'doing the double' of circumnavigating Rùm in kayaks and then climbing all its peaks within a space of 30 hours. It should have been an attainable target but for the thick mist on the second day in which we got lost, spending a 13-hour day in the mountains before abandoning the attempt. This was the occasion on which Michael, who had been given a GPS satellite navigation system as a birthday present, used it for the first time. It showed our altitude as ten feet underwater. Was this, I wondered, some sort of prediction of what was in store for us, or did the little man up there in the satellite, the one watching Michael, simply need a better telescope? To devotees of the Black Art, a GPS is little short of cheating, like using dogs to get to the South Pole. But, isn't it a good thing if more people can experience what the great outdoors has to offer? And, at the same time, new equipment helps raise standards, extending what is possible for those who like to push themselves to the limit. All of which is an old grouch's way of saying that I shall try to restrain myself from accidentally treading on Michael's

GPS. For the time being anyway. I found I had been plying my paddle with a new vigour as I warmed to my argument.

Once, in a thick mist, we set out from Eigg, heading across the eight-mile expanse to Arisaig, riding a rolling, running sea, disappearing into another of those limbo states in which both your departing point and your destination are invisible and where you are mighty glad of company and a compass. In the afternoon of the same day, Archie and I headed off from Arisaig into the enveloping mist, aiming for the comparatively narrow mouth of Loch Moidart. Three hours later, with visibility down to a few feet for the entire crossing and a beam sea throwing us off course, we miraculously arrived slap-bang at the entrance to the loch. Archie was most generous in his praise for my navigation. Naturally, I said nothing to discourage the idea that I was some kind of genius, a cross between a homing-pigeon and Baden Powell, but I knew it was down to sheer luck and a series of errors cancelling each other out.

Some years after this visit to Eigg, I spent a week on the island taking part in a landscape photography course. Before it had been hardly more than a landmark to steer by, easily recognisable by the dramatic profile of the seemingly unscaleable An Sgurr, or it had been a place to land and take a break for an hour before paddling on. I never imagined there could be enough there to keep me enthralled for a whole week, and leaving with the feeling that I needed longer to fully enjoy all that it had to offer. I recall the beautiful woods carpeted with wild garlic, and Laig Bay with its superb views across to Rùm and its fascinating variety of rock formations, a mixture of lava flows and conglomerates, producing pitted moon rocks, veined slabs, hollowed bowls and large squat boulders like dinosaur eggs. Nor shall I forget the magnificent views from the top of An Sgurr (there is an easy way up on its Eastern side), overlooking Muck and Canna, and across to Airsaig and down the length of the Morven Peninsula. Seen from up there, the crossings we had made looked huge and much more daunting than when first studied on the map.

I can't think how it was that I discovered Arisaig so late. I must have been paddling a quarter of a century or so before I became aware of this little gem of a bay with its maze of islands, sandy beaches and its clear shallow waters, through which seals glide. Doug Cooper and George Reid in *Scottish Sea Kayaking: Fifty Great Sea Kayak Voyages* describe it as 'the nearest you will get to paddling in the Caribbean in Scotland'. I would agree with that.

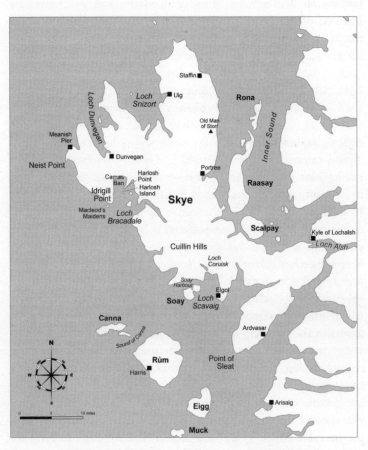

The Isle of Skye, Raasay and surrounding islands

These thoughts and the Skye Boat Song in my head took me across Loch Scavaig, past the beautiful white-sanded Camasunary Bay, to our landing place. We walked the short distance up to Loch Coruisk. After several hours of salt breeze in my face, the scent of bog myrtle and rain-sweet heather was finer than the finest usquebaugh.

Enclosed by perpendicular black bare cliffs, Loch Coruisk lay still and dark, unruffled by the winds against which we had battled. Sir Walter Scott, in his verse novel *The Lord of the Isles* has one of his characters, Bruce, land by boat where we had landed. On reaching Loch Coruisk, he says:

> 'A scene so rude, so wild as this
> Yet so sublime in barreness
> Ne'er did my wandering footsteps press.'

And so, as they say, a good time was had by all. In the days before digital cameras, Ian used to measure how good the outing had been by how many reels of film he'd used, and Archie by how many energy-giving bananas he'd eaten. This had been a three-reel, three-banana day.

A group from the Clydebank and Drumchapel Kayak Club, consisting of Rab, Eva, Colin, Ian and myself, erected our tents at the Sligachan campsite. The hotel, a little way up the road, was a climbers' watering hole, full of ruddy-faced individuals, arms raised, fingers latching onto imaginary holds whose size diminished with each telling. Nobody paid much attention to the small group in the corner, clutching imaginary paddles, facing waves which grew bigger with each pint we downed. The pub reminded me of the Old Dungeon Ghyll Hotel in the Lake District. I don't know if things are the same now, but in the 1950s, for wet weather and evening entertainment, there used to be various difficult traverses round the rough stonewalls of the bar room, and a huge dining table which had to be crossed from end to end via its underside. Clinging to the wall was a stuffed dummy, dressed as a climber. If someone's tale became too tall, too hard to swallow, the dummy would be tipped from its perch.

The following morning we set out from Camas Ban and headed across Loch Bracadale towards Idrigill Point. Our plan was to paddle north along the line of cliffs that stretched all the way to Neist Point. On a previous occasion, the weather being too wild either for paddling or for climbing the peaks, a group of us had walked for about seven miles along the top of these cliffs. Watching the waves pound them we were thankful to be on land. The wind was so strong that you could lean back against it and let it push you up the slope. The waterfalls, which normally tumbled over the edge of the cliffs, were being stopped in mid-air and hurled upwards in huge arching plumes of spray.

We passed close to Harlosh Point and the Piper's Cave, although we didn't stop to check it out. This is the cave into which the piper marched, never to return. As he disappeared into the inky tunnel he exclaimed, 'I doot, I doot I'll ne'er come oot'. The cave is supposed to run underground right across to nearly the other side of Skye. Most of the Skye caves have similar stories with legendary tunnels attached to them. And I seem to recall another such story about Mackinnon's Cave on Mull.

Looking across Loch Bracadale, we could see that the cliffy coastline from Orbost southwards was honeycombed with caves. Just before Idrigill Point we nosed into a deep, dark cavern which boomed and echoed into a blackness we were too frightened to penetrate. As seals swam out beneath us, we backed out, to blink in the sunshine.

Rounding the high, perpendicular cliffs of Idrigill Point, we were greeted by three tall slender maidens – the three spires of MacLeod's Maidens rising out of the sea. Legend has it that, in the fourteenth century, the wife and two daughters of the Chief of the MacLeods were returning to Dunvegan from Harris where the Chief had been mortally wounded in a battle. Here, amongst these stacks that were to take their name, their galley was wrecked and the three women drowned. Another version of the story is that the Mother, as the tallest of the stacks is called, once had three daughters, and that a fourth column formerly existed, which was broken clean across its base during a great storm. Colin spoke about diving around the base of these formations – about the complex system of ravines and gullies down there in which one could easily get lost.

'I'd always thought sky-diving involved jumping out of aeroplanes,' I said.

I questioned Colin further and learned that the west coast of Scotland is rated as one of the best diving areas in the world. It has clean, clear water, wonderfully varied scenery with sheer underwater cliffs and spectacular reefs and enough wrecks to make the coastline a museum of shipping history. Colin said the marine wildlife off the coast of Scotland was every bit as diverse and colourful as places like the Great Barrier Reef, with many kinds of crabs, scallops, starfish, anemones, squirts, sponges, soft corals, urchins, limpets, sea slugs and other species to be found and many more still awaiting discovery in the thick kelp forests. As well as having specific sites and wrecks that were great to dive, the west coast also offers some fabulous drift diving.

'Drift diving? What's that?'

'It's when you let the current carry you along. It uses up less air because you're not exerting yourself so much, which means you can stay submerged for longer.'

'What about the wrecks?'

Colin said that within quarter of an hour we would be above the wreck of the *Urlana*. On September 5th 1943 the Glasgow-built vessel was en route from Buenos Aires to mainland Britain, carrying a cargo of canned meat. In the early hours of the morning she was driven onto the rocks in a storm. The crew was rescued by another ship, but the *Urlana* was pounded by massive waves and broke up, shedding her cargo into the sea – a cargo which was quickly salvaged, despite the dangers, by a local population emboldened by wartime shortages.

'Sounds like a beefed up version of *Whisky Galore*,' Rab said.

For several miles we explored caverns, chambers, tunnels, passed between stacks and through arches and needles' eyes; then more caves and more arches; and unwinding cliffscapes, gothic towers and castle ramparts, with rock geometry and sea sculpture combining to produce an infinite variety of forms.

With Rab's whoop of joy still echoing around one particularly spectacular cave, I remarked, 'So Rab, you enjoy a little spelean adventure now and then?' He denied it hotly, his blush lighting up the darkness, until I explained that spelean meant 'pertaining to caves'.

We were lucky to have with us two such observant and keen-eyed nature-lovers as Rab and Colin. Whereas I paddle along in my own private bubble of thoughts, these two never miss a thing and, thanks to them, we spotted several dolphins, an otter and a minky whale. With evening drawing on, we came ashore at Ramsaig Bay.

The stars were bright. Satellites and falling stars streaked across the sky. The fire, with ample supplies of driftwood, crackled and blazed, and the beam of Neist Point Lighthouse probed the bay with reassuring regularity. Later we baked foil-wrapped potatoes in the red hot ashes. Later still, I shoved an empty beer bottle amongst the ashes. Gradually, the hard glass became soft and plastic, collapsing into itself and twisting into weird shapes. I still use it as a paperweight.

Next day, the feast of caves, arches and cliff scenery continued. Outside of Orkney and (later) Shetland, I have never met such a concentration of caves. At one point we heard a loud crack and the crashing and rumbling of a massive rock fall, but failed to see where the sound had come from.

As we neared the high cliffs of Neist Point – the most westerly point in Skye– Colin told us that another wreck lay below us, one that attracted prolific shoals of fish. This was the *Dora*, built in 1900 in Norway. Bad weather, thick fog, strong tides and a navigational error led to her demise. The fourteen members of the crew took to the lifeboats and escaped. Within a few days the *Dora* was crushed by heavy seas and slid to the bottom.

A sudden hooligan squall rushed amongst us, then died down as quickly as it had sprung up. Almost immediately after that we were battling the tide-race round Neist Point which, like the squall, quickly relented and allowed us to enjoy the last phase at a leisurely pace, soaking in views across the Minch of Lewis and Harris. When we arrived at our destination, Meanish Pier, my knees were stiff after the long paddle. As I struggled to extract myself from my kayak, Rab said, 'I doot, I doot he'll ne'er come oot!'

Chapter 21

Dreamcatcher

Gigha and Iona

Gigha and Iona are two islands I have been drawn to again and again. They are roughly similar in size and shape, both can be circumnavigated by kayak in a day given reasonably good weather, both are reached by fairly short crossings, both can produce challenging conditions and tranquil moments in equal parts, and both have their own special aura about them. Gigha, 'God's Isle', is the most southerly of the Inner Hebrides. It is a joy to go round and a joy to view from afar. I recall one trip along the Knapdale Peninsula between West Loch Tarbert and Loch Caolisport with Gigha filling the southern skyline, its gradually changing profile wedged between a slate sea and a grey sky, striped by alternate shafts of sunlight and columns of cloud-burst. Although it lies only two and a half miles off the Kintyre coast, Gigha's soul definitely belongs to the Hebrides. It feels more remote and wilder than its closeness to the mainland would suggest. Following its rocky, indented skerry-studded coastline is a totally different experience from visiting its lush, fertile interior with its famous gardens and ancient church. Making the crossing in a kayak has produced many a case of 'white knuckle' and subsequent tales in the pub of 'interesting' seas. When elsewhere the sea has been relatively benign, it can be kicking up quite nastily in the Sound of Gigha – partly because of the shallow bottom there and partly because any wind that's going seems to be compressed in the Sound and accelerates to another couple of forces more than has been forecast. Several fellow paddlers I know have opted to take the ferry back to the mainland because of the bad conditions. Usually, no charge is made for this.

I have paddled round it on three or four occasions, either as a longish daytrip or as a fairly leisurely one night camping trip – well, leisurely in theory at least, although it hasn't always worked out that way. There was an exhilarating paddle up the west side, hitching a ride northwards on a rolling green sea that was powered by a following wind and a spring tide on the flood. It was the kind of sea that demanded attention but remained just the right side of the thin line between thrill and anxiety. No eyes for the scenery that day. But on another occasion, going south-wards down the same coastline with only mild opposition from the elements, I was able to enjoy the outlines of Jura and Islay, whiffs of purple against a hazy sky, and the Gigha cliffs, surpris-ingly green and vegetated considering their steepness, with smooth rounded rocks at the north end, becoming more jagged in the south, seals on the outlying rocks, and microlites from the nearby private airstrip swooping overhead like prehistoric birds.

Once, camping in the big sandy bay on the south side of Gigha's Eilean Garbh isthmus in a spot sheltered from a strong south-easterly wind, I pitched my tent on a dry stretch of sand between two smaller bays. As I lay in my sleeping bag I became aware of the sound of lapping water on either side of me becom-ing ever louder. I popped my head out. The expanse of dry sand had shrunk to a strip about ten feet wide – of which my tent occupied the major part. And still the water kept rising well past the calculated time for it to stop. Finally, as I was on the point of a hasty flight, with the sea no more than two feet away to left and right, the tide reached its highest point and lay still.

Next morning, in the same bay, rather than failing to stop rising when it was meant to, the tide failed to rise at all. It just sat there long past the appointed hour for low water, not moving an inch. Surely I couldn't have got my calculations so completely wrong? When I recounted this strange happening to Colin, he told me he'd had exactly the same experience when camping on Gigha. So convinced was he that his tide tables must be inaccurate that he returned to the marina where he'd bought them and demanded his money back. There is a surprisingly small rise and fall of tide on Gigha. The difference between high and low water at spring tide is only about four feet, while during neap tides, a wind from the south can reduce the difference to no more than one foot. The smallness of the tides is due to the main tide flowing in from the Atlantic at a different time from the flood tide flowing out of the Irish Sea, so that the two tides, both of which affect Gigha, counterbalance each other. I suppose the same southerly wind that kept the tidal range so small that morning was also responsible for pushing it up close to my tent the previous night. Or maybe not. To tell the truth I'm still baffled. I console myself with the thought that the unpredictability of the tides in these parts is well known and that they vary enormously according to weather conditions. Of the Grey Dog between Scarba and Lunga it is said that not even the local fishermen can be certain within an hour either side of the predicted time when it will start running. And there are other anomalies, such as the tide running at its fastest in the Sound of Gigha, not in the middle period, but during the last hour and a half before slack water when any unsuspecting person might think it should be tailing off. It's all part of what draws me to Gigha.

§

On this particular return to Iona, Colin, Ian and I approached it from Bunessan, along the north side of the Ross of Mull on a sparkling, spanking day with the orange floats of the fishing nets bobbing in the waves, flashing in the sun like navigation buoys. As we paddled into Camas Tuath bay to investigate an interesting stone building, a man emerged from it and shouted to us, 'I saw you coming and put the kettle on'. The building, he told us, was now a retreat/adventure centre belonging to the Iona Community. Before that it had at various times been a poor house

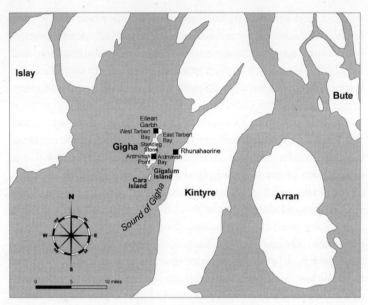

Gigha

(as in a place for destitute people), a salmon fishing base, and housing for the men who quarried the granite needed to build Skerryvore Lighthouse, 30 miles west of the Ross of Mull out in the Atlantic, which was completed in 1844.

Three or four grey seals were swimming in the bay. Our host said there were nearly one hundred thousand grey seals around the Scottish coast. I commented that it must be difficult to count them. Imagine having to start all over again if you lost count! He told us that these days aerial photographs are taken and the number of seals counted from the photograph. A more recent method is to use helicopters fitted with a thermal imaging camera which detects the warmth of a seal's body and can estimate the number of seals within a given area.

Turning south round the headland, we paddled with Iona less than a mile to our right across the Sound of Iona, its white sands, rich greenery and pink abbey delighting the eye. But nearer, on our left and strongly competing for our attention, were pink granite cliffs, islands and skerries with vertical strata jabbing fingers into the sky, flushed and rosy as if bathed in the last rays of a glorious sunset, and yet it was only four in the afternoon. With tide, wind and wave all going our way, we wafted through the Bull Hole, that beautiful passage between mainland Mull and Eileannam Ban, gliding, as if in a dream, through liquid jade. In a moment of serendipity, I was carried past a yacht riding at anchor, named *Dreamcatcher*. According to Native American lore, dream catchers invite good dreams into the drifting mind but trap the bad ones. They are made from bendy twigs, beads and feathers. Here, in this magic corner of the world, my dream-catcher was made of green sea, white sand, bright blue sky and pink rock. At that moment I was supremely happy. I was happy because I was fulfilling a basic human need to stay in contact with the rest of nature and with the spirit of wildness. I believe this to be essential to the sanity of the human species.

The Sound, when we crossed it, treated us to a rolling rhyth-mical motion, which went perfectly with our kayaks and our mood. On another occasion, out in the middle of the Sound, in much rougher seas, Michael said, 'We'd better keep close together here'. Then a wave picked up my kayak and dumped me on top of his deck. 'I didn't mean that close!' he commented.

The variety of miniature cliffs, gorges and inlets along Iona's south-east coastline afforded unceasing interest, as did the grad-ually unfolding curve round the south-west corner of the Ross of Mull with its rugged coastline and spectacular coves, bays and sands. Here lies the island of Erraid which was the land base for the construction of the Dhu Heartach lighthouse which marks the infamous Torran reef twelve miles out to sea. In the period 1800–1854, before the lighthouse was built, thirty ships were wrecked on the reef and over fifty lives lost. The Dhu Heartach lighthouse was completed in 1872 and automated in 1971. While it was being constructed, mountainous waves washed several stone blocks, each weighing two tons, into the sea from a height of 46 feet above sea level. This was another of the many light-houses around the coast designed by Thomas Stevenson. His son, Robert Louis, spent several childhood summer holidays on Erraid. It is said that he based his map of Treasure Island, the one used in the original version of the book, on Erraid.

We had been warned about 'the Boilings', the turbulent water that can be found when going round the bottom end of Iona. Despite arriving there at slack water, the sea in the passages between the small islands was choppy, with a feeling of dark menace about it, and the swell rolling in from the exposed south-west was big enough to make us thankful the wind had dropped. Colin confessed to me later that the sight of Ian putting away his camera as we approached the Boilings had made him distinctly nervous. For Ian to do such a thing was a sure sign of some pretty nasty stuff ahead.

We camped on the flower-rich machair above a sandy bay and walked up to Dun I, which at 300 feet is the highest point on the island. There are few summits in Scotland which can boast such a magnificent view from so lowly a viewpoint. Westward stretched the Atlantic laughing in the breeze under a lingering sun, merging its horizon with the sky and with the distant smudge of Barra Head. Nearer and more to the north lay Tiree and Coll. Some kind of mirage was producing an exact inverted image of Coll which floated above the real island. Directly north, beyond Eigg and Rùm, were the minarets of the Cuillins of Skye. Moving eastwards our gaze took in the mountains of Knoydart, Morar and Mull. Iona, Sacred Heart of the Western Isles.

As we ate our meal in the dusk, a huge orange moon floated up from the south, tempting us to launch our kayaks again and circuit the bay, watching the wet sand gleaming like a sheet of newly fallen snow. Clouds moved in from the west, blotting out the moon. Even so, the night retained a soft glow which reflected off silvered sands, pebbles and polished slabs.

Next morning found us battling northwards into a stiff breeze which threatened to snatch the paddles from our grasp. After struggling round the northern end of Iona, we landed for a rest. A gust caught Ian's paddle, bowling it across the sand, making strange imprints, such as no animal had ever before made on Iona. Behind the beach, grass slopes were ablaze with yellow flowers as in some medieval tapestry. Across the Sound lay Mull. We set out into the teeth of a strong wind, plunging and bucking though a bright green sea, white capped with angels' wings, spray flying off our bows into our faces, Iona now behind us.

More than 70 years ago, Seton Gordon wrote in *Highways and Byways in the West Highlands*:

Iona, remote as it is, begins to feel the influence of this modern age. The Gaelic language is dying out. No longer does the old ferryman, Coll McLean, sail out from Fionphort in his well-tried skiff, braving the winter storms with reefed sails and carrying the mail to Iona ... Yet the Atlantic, mother and guardian of this isle, remains both unchanged and ever changing. The waves roll into the caverns as they did in the day of Columba, and the great grey seals, which were the saint's special care, still swim in the boiling surf of Port a' Churaich.

Chapter 22

The Realms Of Night

Night paddling

I have mentioned elsewhere in this book the delights of night paddling: a night on Loch Lomond, a late return across the bay to Helensburgh, slipping my kayak into the pink dawn water on the margins between day and night . . . There have been so many magic moments when other senses are alerted and when familiar places become new and exciting and utterly transformed. My fascination with the realms of night goes back a long way. Age six: my father meeting my mother, brother and self off the boat at Bombay, driving us through the night across the Deccan Plateau – the blazing red eyes of packs of jackals caught in the car's headlights, the luminous orbs of the buffalo, the singing of frogs that filled the soft scented air, the distant flicker of light-ning, columns of illuminated dust raised by a passing truck, a huge orange sun sliding slowly above the horizon. Age thirteen: on my first youthful camping trips with friends, becoming aware, in a way one never does indoors, of sunsets, starry nights, the travelling moon and the calls of nocturnal animals. Age seven-teen: at the tiller of *Grakle*, my father's ketch, crossing from Dartmouth to Cherbourg at two o'clock in the morning, the phosphorescence on the crests of the waves, stars falling across the sky, the pool of light from the compass-well like an oasis in the darkness. As a student at Cambridge: climbing the ancient buildings at night – shinning up drainpipes or ornately carved and gargoyled facades, traversing steeply tiled roofs with the silent streets below, leaping across gaps between one building and another (one leap was best not done sober, so it was thought, or you hesitated fatally at the crucial moment), lying beneath the big clock on the college tower, a second moon in the sky, as it boomed out the midnight hour.

As well as discovering night paddling, I discovered night walking. There have been climbs in the Alps which started at three or four in the morning to cross a glacier before snow bridges over deep crevasses softened in the sun and collapsed under our weight. Usually the first hour roped together passes in silence, breath hissing into the crisp air, crampons crunching across moon-blue ice, metal axes ringing. The body yearns for the comfort of a warm sleeping bag and yet there is nowhere else one would rather be than there, under the stars, with the high peaks catching the first rays of the sun.

And there was the moonlight ascent of Ben Ime with Martin – he who came on many of the earlier paddles with me. It was the coldest spell Scotland had experienced for 40 years. Pale shrouded ridges haunted the skyline, the lochs lay in a frozen trance. The mountains held their breath, their rushing burns iron-gripped. We crossed wind-rippled, moon-dappled surfaces of sheer delight and pearl-encrusted acres which sparkled in a way never seen by day. When the moon set we dug a snow hole and waited for the coming of the light. Due south, Greenock, Gourock and Dunoon were twinkling bracelets on a black velvet coast. The Cloch Point Lighthouse blinked steadily, and far down the Firth of Clyde, Ailsa Craig's beam made silver pinpricks in the dark. Slowly, night's ashen shapes rekindled in dawn's fire. We stretched stiff limbs and wandered in disbelief over fields of crimson snow towards our blood red peak.

A Greenland summer offers an entirely different sort of night adventure, if you can call it night in a land where the sun doesn't set for several months. We would sometimes paddle until midnight and eat our 'evening' meal at one or two in the morning, still able to see with comparative ease. The following is an extract from my book *Fallen Pieces of the Moon* about a short walk at three o'clock of an Arctic morning:

> I walked a little way up the slope and sat in the springy scrub. A light breeze had sprung up again: just the right amount to keep the mosquitoes and other bugs at bay. Clouds, like slowly drifting windflowers, bloomed in shades of pink. To the east the higher snow slopes blushed at the touch of the low lying sun and steep rock faces glowed like molten lava as though, any moment, they would pour in rivers of scarlet and gold into a sea bejewelled with floating rubies.

Two night paddles embedded in my mind were both unplanned. The first was when, on the way to Oban, a wheel came off the trailer. By the time it was fixed it was pretty late although still light since it was close to midsummer. On an impulse, Ian and I decided not to bother putting up the tent, but simply to launch and paddle round Kerrera, down the outside and back up the inner passage. This was the kind of trip one does 'once in a blue moon'. So it was fitting that the next full moon, although still a week away, was indeed a blue moon – which is defined as being either the second full moon in one month, or the third full moon in a (three month) season which contains four full moons.

The blazing sky, the long, lingering twilight shot with gradually bruising clouds, the silhouettes of the Mull mountains against an orange glow and the long vista, in the simmer dim, down the Firth of Lorn with the Garvellachs, Colonsay and Jura clearly visible, and the crackling fire when we stopped in the darkest hour, then skimming through the softly approaching dawn in a kayak named *Dawn Treader* – these things are now a part of me.

The second was on Loch Morar. The day had been made memorable by a glorious rainbow which arched the loch and the roaring of stags, echoing in the high glens on either side of us. Later though, it clouded over and began to drizzle. The five of us (the usual Famous Five) beached our kayaks at the head of the loch quite late in the day only to find that the bothy we had planned to use was locked and barred. We had no tents with us and it was a cold, damp evening. Sleeping out in the open was not an inviting prospect. With night closing in on us we decided to paddle back to where we had left the cars. It was a murky, overcast night. Fortunately Loch Morar has very few powered boats on it likely to run us down in the dark. Although it is not mandatory in UK waters for kayaks to carry navigation lights (red lights on port side, green lights on starboard side, white lights fore and aft), and although we had not foreseen this turn of events, most of us had equipment for night paddling permanently stowed in our bags. Between us we could muster a strobe light for switching on if something big and menacing was bearing down on us, three or four red lights for clipping to the stern or the back of a life jacket, the same number of head lamps for use when reading a map or doing something fiddly, and a couple of powerful spotlight torches for picking out hazards and potential landing places; and all of us had strips of reflective tape on our decks and at least one white flare each which could be fired off to alert a big boat to our presence – unlike a red flare, a white flare is not a distress signal and hopefully will not trigger a rescue operation. Even with this equipment it was all too easy to lose touch with each other and we resorted to continually shouting out a roll call of our names: 'Robin here!' 'Michael here!' Loch Morar is quite shallow in places, with sharpish rocks inches beneath the surface or lurking just high enough to be mistaken for a black lump of water. A breeze had sprung up, causing waves to swirl around the protruding rocks, sometimes warning us of their presence, sometimes not.

When the shallows became too dangerous we would move out into the middle of the loch. In the dark, with the shores invisible, I was seized by a strong sense of the inky black depths beneath me. Loch Morar, at over 1,000 feet deep, is the deepest loch in Scotland, deeper than Loch Ness, and deeper than the sea for 150 miles out into the Atlantic until the edge of the shelf is reached beyond St Kilda. If ever there was a night for encountering Morag, the resident monster, this was it. Morag was involved in perhaps one of the most frightening and physical encounters of any British lake monster. In August 1969 two men reported that they were fishing on the loch in a motor cruiser when they became aware of a loud splashing behind them. They said they saw a creature in the water, about 30 feet long, which deliberately rammed the boat side-on. One of the fishermen grabbed his shot-gun and fired at the creature. They described it as having dirty brown rough skin, three large black humps and a snake-like head. Much to their relief, the creature slowly slipped back under the water after it had been shot at. Morag has been seen on several other occasions and, if not for the loch's remoteness (there is no road around the Loch), there would probably be many more sightings.

Out in the middle it was difficult to see where we were in relation to the shore or to keep track of our progress. Anxious not to pass our parked cars without knowing it, we moved closer to the shore again. I read somewhere that the retina in our eyes which best translate low-level light into nerve impulses are on the edges of our pupils. We therefore see objects better at night if we look 5 to 20 degrees away from them. I think, possibly, we do this slight turning of the head back and forth when peering into the dark instinctively. My optician, on the other hand, says this is rubbish. Her exact words were: 'In practical terms, it doesn't make a blind bit of difference!'

I kept losing sight of the others, or narrowly missing things that jumped out of the gloom without warning. Colin, who seemed to have catlike vision, internal radar and several extra senses, led the way. But for him I would have rammed into the almost invisible obstacles several times over – jagged things which stuck out of the water like a monster's spine. In the dark, one stretch of tree-lined shore looked much like another, and the same went for beaches, inlets and just about everything else.

Passages between islands so easily navigated by day became nightmares of uncertainty on the way back, our tension compounded by unnerving rustlings and scurryings amongst the nearby undergrowth. Finally, Colin's torch picked out a beach and beyond it our parked cars. I don't know whether it was the long day paddling down the length of Loch Morar and back again, or the stress of concentrating so hard in the darkness, but we were all strangely disorientated when we got out of our kayaks, staggering about the road, unable to walk a straight line. No, we weren't drunk, except with relief and with a deep satisfaction that we had turned what could have been a dismal ending to the day into a memorable experience.

Chapter 23

Other Worlds Are Possible

Shetland

Thursday

Early one July morning at Lerwick in the Shetland Isles, two cars weighed down by a total of five kayaks and mountains of gear, rolled off the overnight ferry from Aberdeen. At this point we were just north of the bottom end of Greenland, about level with Bergen in Norway and closer to the Arctic Circle than we were to London. The Scottish Mountaineering Club Guide describes the Shetlands as having 'the finest and most striking variety of magnificent sea-cliffs to be found in the whole of the British Isles'. Michael, Ian, Colin and Archie had all kayaked in the Shetlands before, some of them several times. They regaled me with tales of what I had missed, of unbelievable luck with long unbroken spells of good weather; they showed me photographs of the magnificent sea caves on the exposed side of Papa Stour – possibly the most impressive in the British Isles – which can only be entered on the rare days when the swell isn't thundering into them and which, of course, they had the good fortune to be able to do. Tom Smith, the well known Shetland kayak guide whom we met up with later, is of the opinion that going round Papa Stour is one of the best day trips to be had anywhere. The amazing cliffs on its western side include Christie's Hole, reckoned to be the finest sea cave in Europe, and Hole o' Broadie, a 300-metre-long tunnel, thought to be the fourth longest sea cave in the world. And my lucky companions, whom I was going off rapidly

by the minute, eagerly plied me with descriptions of the spectacular stretch of cliffs, stacks and caves at Eshaness, which they
all agreed must be one of the finest sea kayak routes in Europe.
Apart from being jealous as hell and sick as a parrot that I had
missed all this, I didn't believe that such good weather could
possibly strike twice in the same place. This far north we had to
accept that we might not get even one day of paddling out of the
ten we planned to be here for. We were going to spend a couple
of nights in a hostel near the tip of South Mainland and then
move north to the island of Yell where we had rented a house for
a week.

We drove in thick mist to a point half way down the east side
of South Mainland where we set out to paddle round the island
of Mousa. Before long we reached a point, symbolic for a group
whose average age was well into the fifties, where the mainland
had faded from sight but the promised island had not yet
appeared. Most of the caves were long and narrow, forcing us to
ship our paddles because there was no room to wield them, and
to propel ourselves forward by pushing against the walls with
our hands. Although we all had torches, I still found myself feeling for something solid in the dark, leaning too far and wildly
groping at thin air as the walls receded or a swell nudged me
beyond their reach with no paddle in hand for support. Not
surprisingly, one of our party capsized. In a narrow restricted
space, in semi-darkness, with kayaks and paddles banging
against each other, against the walls and against the roof, the
rescue wasn't exactly a model of slick efficiency. These were caves
full of treasure – shoals of tiny translucent fish; a luminous virid-
ian pool illuminated by a shaft of light where the cave roof had
partly collapsed; pink sea anemones on red rock; blow holes
through which the swell snorted and escaped in explosive gusts.

Our lunch break was taken near the famous broch of Mousa,
an Iron Age fort built somewhere between 100 BC and AD 100. It
is a conical dry stone tower, tapering slightly towards the top,
with walls about 15 feet thick at the base. Above the base the

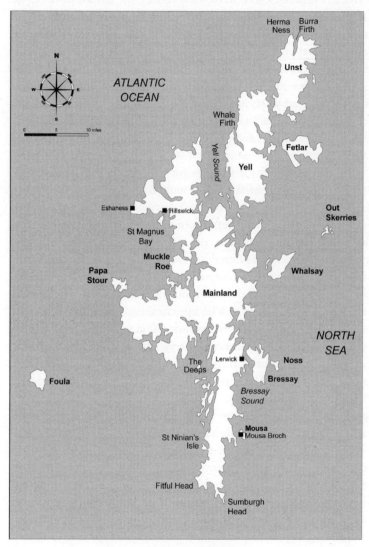

The Shetland Islands

walls are double with a staircase in between winding upwards, which is probably what enabled it to be built without the aid of scaffolding. The Mousa broch is the tallest and best preserved tower of its kind. Whereas no other broch now stands higher than 20 feet, this one is over 40 feet high. When making any stone structure relied on collecting loose stones for miles around, it is no wonder that, in other more populated areas, the brochs, Roman forts and other ancient buildings were dismantled by the local populace and used for other purposes. Little is known about the race that built these brochs. Whoever they were they have disappeared and nobody is really sure who they were, where they came from or what language they spoke. The view from the top of the tower must have been much the same 2,000 years ago as it is now and the tides would have run the same for the ancient fishermen in their coracles as they did for us in our kayaks.

Resuming our circumnavigation of Mousa, we saw a lamb marooned on a narrow ledge at the mouth of a cave, its plaintive bleats echoing into the darkness. We discussed whether to attempt a rather risky rescue operation and decided against it, convincing ourselves that at low tide the lamb would probably be able to walk out of the cave to safety. The coast curved so gently that, in the mist, I had no sensation of going round an island. I was quite surprised to come upon the same cave entrance that I'd seen several hours earlier.

We had arranged to stay in a böd at Scatness. A böd is, or was, a building used to house fishermen and their gear during the fishing season. This one, by the name of Betty Mouat's Böd had been converted into a self-catering hostel. On the way there we were held up at crossing gates of an unusual kind – the main road south goes straight across the runway of Sumburgh Airport and we waited as a plane took off, climbing into the sky right opposite us.

Betty Mouat became famous when, in January 1886, as a frail 60-year-old, she found herself adrift in the North Sea on the smack *Columbine* with no crew on board. It was a bitter cold day when Betty was the sole passenger on the *Columbine* bound for Lerwick. She was traveling from her home in Scatness up the coast to town to sell her knitting. The only food she had with her was a bottle of milk and some biscuits. The voyage should have taken under three hours. But a storm blew up. In rising seas the skipper was washed overboard. The mate and the deckhand jumped into a small boat in an attempt to rescue him, but he was lost, and they were unable to catch up with the drifting *Columbine*. Eight days later the *Columbine* smashed into the Norwegian coast, three hundred miles to the northeast. The chances of survival in a winter storm would have been bleak for any person, let alone a 60 year old woman, but Betty did survive and lived on in the Shetlands until the age of 93.

Friday
Bigton Bay, facing north, and St Ninian's Bay, facing south, share the same beach − a fairly unusual feature known as an ayre or tombolo. We set off from St Ninian's, aiming to round Fitful Head and land not far from Betty Mouat's Böd. We crossed the green, translucent bay, the sandy seabed briefly darkened by the shadows of skimming birds. The mist gently enfolded us, receiving us into a Chinese watercolour painting of soft, blurred outlines where cliffs, stacks and headlands became subtle, merging qualities of grey. Tall pointed stacks, arches like the eye of a needle, narrow passages, deep dark caves, tunnels which emerged further along the coast − all given added interest by a long, slow swell which remained benign until you made your move, whereupon it inevitably let loose an extra breaking, snarling surge of power. This, for Shetland, was a gentle swell. Even so, its encounter with the cliffs and rocks and skerries was thrilling to behold. We were in a zone where the ocean slanted upwards, piling up and up against the first obstructions it had met in thousands of miles. Then it withdrew, pouring in rivers, waterfalls and cataracts off the rocks, cascading over ledges, churning the sea into

foaming whites, blues and greens. While I was rounding a little group of mist-girt outcrops, one of these surges swept in completely engulfing the lesser outcrops of twelve feet or so. The larger outcrop had, running up its steep outer side, a wide groove or gut. Water rushed up this, a river in full torrent going the wrong way, spouting and spraying in the air as it reached the top. While attempting a very narrow passage between two high walls – one that nobody else dared try – Archie's paddle was knocked from his grasp. 'He's in trouble!' I thought. Then a swell funnelling down the passage picked up the paddle and carried it back into his grasp.

We skirted the margins of this unpredictable chaos, sometimes becoming too embroiled with it for comfort. The ocean would take its slow, slumbering breaths for ten minutes or more before heaving a huge sigh. I was constantly surprised by how far it sucked and drained out again at these turbulent times, exposing unexpected rocks beneath me. It always seemed that, rather than the sea receding and uncovering hidden dangers, the rocks were actively rearing up out of the depths like sharp-fanged, roaring monsters. On one occasion, Ian and Archie took an inner passage, sheltered by a line of rock at least fifteen feet high, only to find the swell leaping these outer defences and crashing down upon them, bouncing off the opposite walls, turning what seconds before had been a peaceful passageway into a seething cauldron.

More cliffs – writhing twisting grained and crystalline strata, big black angular blocks, smooth red slabs. A float, the kind that holds up fishing nets, was jammed into a crack some sixty or seventy feet up the cliff. What size of wave, we wondered, must have hurled it that high? The winter storms here are notorious. The Clyde Cruising Club's sailing directions for Shetland say, 'No small sailing vessel should be in these waters from October to March.' I have read a description of the mareel in a winter storm (mareel is the Shetland word for the phosphorescence which glows like a pool of fire under the dip of an oar) – Bluemill

Sound on a winter night, when spring tides of ten knots roar into the teeth of a 90 mile-an-hour gale, and the seething ocean is aflame with cold fire.

Then yet more caves – one boomed steadily like a drum beat, the source of which was the surf pounding the beach of a connected cave, the sound amplified in the high vaulted chamber. In another cave, the darkness around us exploded into a frenzy of thrashing, splashing echoing noise as a large seal swam out close underneath us.

We reached Fitful Head only just in time before 'the roost' round the headland gained velocity and started kicking up. Just east of Fitful Head, at Garth's Ness, is where the oil tanker *Braer* laden with Norwegian crude oil went aground in a storm in January 1993. Luckily, it was not quite the disaster for the local environment and wildlife that it could have been because some of the worst storms seen that century pounded the coast for days on end, dispersing the leaking oil. Within two years the winter storms had crushed and compressed this huge vessel and sent it to the bottom.

Once past the developing roost, we relaxed and paddled towards our final beach in the gentlest swell of the day. We had relaxed too soon. As we neared the beach, we could see surf breaking onto it. The harmless swell was picking up speed and height as it reached the shallow bay, tripping over itself and crashing onto the shore. Ian was first to attempt the landing. The surf picked up man and kayak and hurled them sideways up the beach, sending them rolling over and over like a child rolling down a hill, only they were going up the way. Gulp. Umm . . . Whose turn next? Colin bided his time, looking over his shoulder, trying to choose a moment when the surf had died down a bit. It worked and he landed safely.

'Me next!' I shouted.

It was easier for Colin and Ian (albeit a rather subdued Ian) to watch the waves that were coming up behind me and shout from the beach when I should start my run in:

'Go! Now! Now!'

As soon as I started I could see from the horrified expressions on their faces that they had made a mistake and that the largest wave yet was bearing down on me. I was flung sideways but managed to lean in to the wave, cushioning its crest under my raised arm, almost resting on it as it sped me towards the beach. I arrived still upright and was on the point of congratulating myself on a successful landing, when the undertow started to drag me out again. Colin dashed into the water and hauled me and my kayak up the beach. Final result: Surf 2½, Kayakers 2½.

Saturday

We spent the Saturday moving up to our rented house at Grimster on Yell, overlooking Whale Firth. A detour saw us scoffing coffee and cakes at the café attached to the Hillswick Wildlife Sanctuary on North Mainland. In a strangely old fashioned, dark room was a sign: 'Other worlds are possible'. As we wolfed down plates of delicious homemade cakes, we discussed our next trip to the Shetlands. There is so much here for a kayaker to do, so many wonders, so many parts of it still to explore and so many places worthy of visiting again and again that we decided to make the Shetlands a regular fixture on the list for our annual 'big trip', and to come back to it every second year if we could.

We were surprised when, rather than paying a set price for the coffee and cakes, we were asked to give a donation – whatever we felt we wanted to give. According to the pamphlet I picked up, in 1976, the year that work began on the Sullom Voe Oil Terminal, Jan Bevington took over the Booth, the oldest pub in Shetland. Two years later she found a young Common Seal washed up on the beach directly in front of the Booth. Jan looked after it in her front garden. Word rapidly spread throughout the isles and that summer six more sick seals were brought to the Booth to be cared for and released back to the wild. So it was that the Hillswick Wildlife Sanctuary was born. It struggled to keep going, but when the oil tanker, the *Braer*, went aground a huge rescue operation for Shetland's wildlife was mounted and animal welfare groups and volunteers from all over the world descended on the Booth. The *Braer* disaster changed life at the Booth for good. Jan closed the ailing pub business to devote herself to caring for wildlife. One unusual beneficiary of the sanctuary was a seven-foot long leatherback turtle which had become entangled in fishing nets. It weighed more than one ton and was reckoned to be at least a hundred years old.

Sunday

We paddled up Whale Firth and round the north end of Yell to Cullivoe, having left a car there before we started. The general remoteness of this firth made it a good place for German subma- rines to hide and shelter during World War I. Now this remote- ness is one reason for the land area at the north-west end of Whale Firth being a RSPB reserve where breeding species include the red-throated diver, the red-breasted merganser, golden plover, eider, merlin, curlew, snipe, lapwing, arctic and great skuas, dunlin, great black-backed gull, raven, twite, and wheatear.

My outstanding memory of this day is of one spectacularly heavy cloudburst, which lasted for nearly an hour. The surface of the water, as far as the eye could see, was pearl encrusted with raindrops which flattened the waves and turned the seascape into something akin to a loudly hissing, undulating, frost-covered prairie. My deck, my clothing, my raised hood drummed with the onslaught of the rain which found its way up sleeves and down my neck in such quantities that I could feel water slopping about inside the cockpit. For about two hours after the heavens opened, massive volumes of water poured over the cliffs. Gushing torrents filled every gulley and groove, sluiced across slabs, became thundering waterfalls at every overhang. As if in imita- tion of this superabundance of flowing water, veins of quartz, ten feet wide or more in places, streaked and criss-crossed the cliffs. We sheltered in one of the many sea caves, having first to pass through the mini-Niagara which screened its entrance. The interior of the cave was noticeably cooler than outside. Lodged high at the back of the cave was something that looked very like an old World War II sea mine.

The rugged cliff-girt coastline offered nowhere to stop, but more than compensated for this with its display of pyramidal stacks, pointing fingers, serrated edges and high narrow canyons winding through these weird formations. Finally, we found a beautiful beach with grassy slopes and a burn shouting joyously in full spate. And the sun came out.

In the sparsely populated northern part of Yell, roads that conveniently run down to a beach are hard to find. Thus it was that, at the end of the day, we had to carry our kayaks up a steep pebbly beach, over a fence and across a field to a track from which Michael and Colin walked several miles to the only place where it had been possible to leave the car. While the rest of us waited in the rain, which had started again, I lay face up in the long wet grass with salt rivers running past my lips tasting of the sea.

Monday
The unanimous vote was for a day off. Michael and Colin went fishing. Ian stayed in the house and . . . I can hardly bring myself to write this . . . and did office work on his laptop. Archie and I elected to walk along the cliff tops.

It was a beautiful fresh day with sky and sea in motion, clouds billowing, the white bog cotton fluttering, surf flinging high on the skerries. For once we were looking at the stacks and seabirds from above. Rabbit burrows abounded on the grassy cliff tops, putting in mind something I'd read: during World War II Shetland was a seaplane base and an outpost for the radar early warning system. It was the first place in the British Isles upon which a German bomb fell. The bomb killed a rabbit which German propaganda inflated into the sinking of a cruiser. Later the RAF dropped the rabbit over enemy territory addressed to Field-Marshal Goering.

That night we had freshly caught sea trout as a starter for our meal.

Tuesday

On this day, joining the usual suspects, were Tom Smith, Shetland's well-known professional kayak guide, and Mavis, a retired teacher and member of Shetland Kayak Club. Mavis took one look at us and said, 'The five of you look like an illustrated history of kayak clothing.'

It was true. Representing the early days was Archie sporting his old rugby vest and hill walking jacket; the next stage of evolution was represented by me clad in a wet-suit. Higher up the ladder were Colin and Ian, wearing the bottom and top halves respectively of dry suits that were last year's model to say the least. At the top of the tree was Modern Michael zippered into the latest snazzy, all breathing, all dancing, all-in-one dry suit. This prompted some impressive old-timer talk from Archie and myself in which we left the soft, greenhorn youngsters in no doubt that men really were men in the good old days, when you paddled bare-chested and struck matches on your stubbly chin.

About a year after this meeting with Tom, the book he co-authored with Chris Jex, *The Northern Isles: Orkney and Shetland Sea Kayaking* was published. Reading this excellent and comprehensive guide brought home to us what a tiny part of the coastline of both Orkney and Shetland we had explored, and the extent of the thrills and pleasures yet to come.

The plan last night had been to take the car ferry over to Unst, launch from its northern end and go round Muckle Flugga and Out Stack, the most northerly islands in the British Isles. But the forecast wasn't good. A force five was blowing from the east. The seas would be big, that is to say, enormous, out there. We decided that at least we would drive up to the launch point and see what it looked like. It looked terrifying. So we opted for a stretch of coast along Unst's westerly, more sheltered side. Even so, we had to plug into a stiff breeze. The swell was there again, breathing in and out, swashing, swirling and cascading, making Jacuzzi pools, hypnotic and endlessly fascinating. I was deep in conversation with Mavis when suddenly I found myself upside down – that swell again! The water beneath me had simply disappeared, leaving me to fall off the edge of a steep-sided rock. It would have made a good story if I could say that when I rolled up I finished the sentence which had been so rudely interrupted. In fact I was too busy spluttering, blowing seawater out of my nostrils and exclaiming in wonder that my sunglasses were still on my face to do any such thing.

Yesterday, a sizeable pod of killer whales had been spotted in the area. Killer whales, or orcas, although small compared to some other species of whales, are the oceans' top predator and the largest predators of mammals ever known. They hunt in groups using team tactics and have been known to attack a blue whale, the biggest animal living on our planet today. We speculated about what we would do if they menaced us. Raft up and have our flares ready to frighten them off if necessary, perhaps. Or let them have a taste of Archie, the oldest and stringiest amongst us, so that they would give up in disgust. Actually, we would almost certainly have been quite safe. Despite rumours to the contrary, killer whales do not normally attack human beings. Originally they were known as 'whale killers' because they attacked other whales, but over time this became twisted into 'killer whales'. In Scottish waters they feed mainly on fish, seals and squid. However, there are accounts from the Inuit of orcas attacking them in their kayaks. Perhaps the fact that the Inuit used skin boats is a significant factor. Knowing that orcas are frightened of walruses, the Inuit would roll upside down in their kayaks and imitate the bellowing grunts of a walrus to scare them off.

Wednesday
The weather forecast predicted a north-westerly wind, force five. We should get sufficient shelter, we reckoned, if we paddled down

the east side of Yell, starting from Mid Yell Voe where the islands of Hascosay and Fetlar would protect us if the wind became more northerly. We were wrong. Almost from the start there was a strong wind at our backs and a rolling sea that crossed an incoming swell.

We visited some caves along the way. On day one I was popping in and out of every cave we passed. Now, on day seven, I wasn't bothering with the small ones. I had become thoroughly spoilt and satiated. Had this stretch of coastline been on the Scottish mainland we would have been wildly enthusiastic about it, visiting it again and again, but here it wasn't fully appreciated amongst so many other riches. Only the really biggest and deepest caves had become worthy of exploration.

The sea was manageable, but only just. And then it got worse. Rounding Heoga Ness at the southern end of Yell, not only was the swell bigger, but it was bouncing back off the headland. My kayak was being thrown all over the place in a nasty, chunky, chaotic sea without any rhythm to it. I tried to look relaxed and nonchalant like the others did. Or were they pretending too? I had been in more turbulent seas than this and not felt nearly so nervous. I tried to think why. Part of the trouble, I think, was that mine was one of the lighter kayaks and, since it was a daytrip, it wasn't fully loaded and was bouncing about on top of the waves rather than carving through them. Also, as a precaution, I had put on my wet-suit, not something I normally do unless the paddling promises to be fairly challenging, and this was causing me to overheat and become hot and bothered instead of staying cool and calm. Was I simply having an off day, or – the conclusion I was trying to avoid – loosing my nerve with the advancing years?

Friday
The Wednesday trip had taken a lot out of everyone, so Thursday was declared another rest day. Since Saturday was set aside for cleaning the house, packing up, driving south and catching the

ferry back to the mainland, today, Friday, was our last chance to have a shot at Muckle Flugga and Out Stack. The wind was force three westerly, edging to four. A force four in the Shetlands can seem a lot more than elsewhere. We decided to paddle up Burra Firth and if it didn't look too bad from the top end, go for it.

Again we took the car ferry across to Unst and drove the length of the island. There was time to spare because we didn't want to be out in the middle until near slack water at noon when the clash between the westerly wind and the tide meeting it head on would be at a minimum. We looked at the little Shetland ponies and at the sheep grazing by the roadside. I have heard it said that the unsurpassed fineness of Shetland wool is due to the poor quality of the grazing. If the sheep are transferred to good grass, their wool becomes coarse. We stopped and took photographs of the most northerly bus shelter in the British Isles – not very exciting, you might think, but this is like no other bus shelter. It even has its own website. A local schoolboy has adopted it and furnished it with tables, an easy chair, cushions, a TV set, paintings, potted plants and flowers.

This time I took the precaution of loading my near-empty kayak with boulders selected from the garden of our rented house. What, I had asked myself, if the launch site is sandy or has no boulders of suitable size or shape? It was only after the trip was over that the obvious solution occurred to me. The one thing you can guarantee will be easy to find at any launch place is seawater. Which is why I now always take a couple of empty water cans and several plastic milk containers and am liable to translate the wind force etc. into gallons. One of my companions commented, rather unkindly I thought, that I didn't need extra ballast since my veteran kayak was already weighed down by umpteen unskilled repairs employing tons of unnecessary fibreglass and resin.

Looking north to the last headlands on mainland Britain, with the empty North Atlantic beyond, it was easy to imagine that this might have been the Ultima Thule of the ancient Greeks, the northernmost habitable region of the world. On ancient maps Thule usually appears north or north-west of England and Ireland or in the northernmost parts of Asia. It has been associated with early reports of Iceland, or the Shetland Islands, but could have been Trondheim in Norway, or even southern Greenland. To medieval geographers, Ultima Thule simply meant a distant, mysterious place beyond the boundaries of the known world. Well, at that precise moment Out Stack seemed like that sort of place.

A large cavern at the north-easterly corner of Burra Firth enticed us into its depths. We could just see its far end opening onto the other side of the headland. Inside its vaulted, dark, dripping interior the water was decidedly jobbly (that is to say jumping about and wobbly) – unsettling when you can't see it properly. Too late we became aware that at the exit on the exposed side of the headland, the sea was battering the rocks and flinging skywards. We paddled furiously through the danger zone, hoping not to be unlucky with a breaking wave, whooping in triumph as we headed out to Muckle Flugga.

The swell was largish but friendly and my extra ballast was definitely making a difference. We paddled along the inner side of the chain of islands of which Muckle Flugga (called North Unst until 1964) with its tall lighthouse at the top, is the biggest, highest and most easterly. Towards the westerly end the cliffs were white with bird droppings and the sky so thick with gannets that we were amazed they never collided.

Landing on Muckle Flugga (which translates as 'big steep-sided island') in a swell is not easy. Most boats only attempt it in calm weather. The trick was to get the timing right. One by one we waited for the right moment, then made a quick dash to a slot between two rocks at the base of the cliff, followed by a wild scramble to get out before the next big wave crashed in. After man-hauling the kayaks up some big boulders to put them out of reach of the breaking swell, we climbed 200 feet to the base of the lighthouse, up flights of aluminium stairs fixed to the cliff beside the original rough stairway cut into the rock. The lighthouse is yet another built by Thomas Stevenson. It was completed in 1858 and was manned until 1995 when it was automated. Before that a temporary lighthouse 50 feet in height had been erected. Although its base was 200 feet above the sea, in the winter gales the waves not only broke heavily on the tower, but ran up the sides and burst open the door of the dwelling room, as well as carrying off a large section of the stone wall around the light-house. As a result of this, the permanent tower was made higher than originally planned. Robert Louis Stevenson stayed for a short time on Unst when his father brought him to visit the light-house in 1869. Some people say it is no coincidence that the map of Treasure Island in the original version of the book looks very like Unst. Now, where have I heard that before? Oh yes, wasn't the same claim made for the island of Erraid, off the Ross of Mull?

From the lighthouse we looked across the tide-ripped stretch of water to the Hermaness peninsula of Unst, much of which is a nature reserve. On its tall cliffs is one of the UK's largest puffin colonies (puffins are known locally as Tammie Nories), with around 25,000 breeding pairs. It was from here that the great skua made a comeback. Geat skuas (known in the Shetlands as Bonxies) are sometimes called 'flying pirates' because they force other birds to drop their latest meal. By the beginning of the 20th century only two or three pairs of great skuas were known to exist in the world and they were here at Hermaness. Now, thanks to protection, they have recovered their numbers. Shetland has about one third of the world's great skua population and they have now spread to Orkney, the north of mainland Scotland, Iceland, Norway and the Faroe Isles.

Then, on to Out Stack, a small roundish rocky island a few hundred metres to the north of Muckle Flugga, the full stop at the end of Britain. Its sides were too steep and the swell too big to land. Instead each of us threw a pebble onto it, so that some-thing of us at least, had touched the most northerly extremity of our homeland. As we rounded Out Stack there was a thrill in knowing that, at that moment, we were the most northerly people in the British Isles. If I paddled east my first landfall would be Norway, going west across the North Atlantic it would be Greenland, while to the north nothing but ocean lay between me and the North Pole.

Postscript

There are so many more magical places yet to be explored. Several lifetimes of voyaging and venturing. Then there's the sea itself which performs a million miracles a minute and which would take an eternity to know in all its moods. Emerson said, 'People do not grow old, they become old when they stop growing.' Over the horizon is the Land of the Ever Young, a land whose treasures are a sense of awe and wonder, physical and mental renewal and spiritual growth; a land where, for the Argonauts who quest after it, there is to be found the Golden Fleece.